Primary Professional Development

Primary School Drugs Education Handbook

Adrian King

Editor: Karen Westall
Illustrations: Eric Jones
Layout artist: Suzanne Ward
Cover design: Ed Gallagher

British Library Cataloguing in Publication Data. A catalogue record for this book is available from the British Library.

First published 2000 by Folens Limited, Dunstable and Dublin.
Folens Limited, Albert House, Apex Business Centre, Boscombe Road, Dunstable, LU5 4RL, England.

ISBN 1 86202 649–1

Contents

Introduction

This book is written in response to a changing climate in drugs education which gives greater recognition to the contribution of primary schools. The government White Paper 'Tackling Drugs to Build a Better Britain' includes in its aim, 'Prevention should start early, with broad life-skills approaches at primary school, and built on over time with appropriate programmes for young people as they grow older ...'. It goes on to support activities which 'teach young people from the age of five upwards – both in and out of formal education settings – the skills needed to resist pressure to misuse drugs, including a more integrated approach to Personal, Social and Health Education in schools, and with particular reference to the ... DfEE guidance.' This guidance, published in November 1998, states 'Primary schools ... have a vital role to play in preparing pupils for situations they meet in and out of school throughout their school lives and beyond.'

The Primary School Drugs Education Handbook addresses the world of drugs and its relationship to primary education today. It challenges common myths, replacing them with a more balanced picture of the drugs people use, details of their legal status, an account of their effects, the dangers and traps they can present to the unwary, and their place in the culture of today's growing population of school children. It goes on to explore the primary school's role in responding to the phenomenon of drug use both through educational input and through the way it manages drugs that come on to school premises for any reason.

There is no need for the very word 'drugs' to strike fear into our hearts. We hear news that drugs are available on street corners and that younger and younger children are involved, yet drug-taking is not a new phenomenon. It has been with us since the dawn of civilisation.

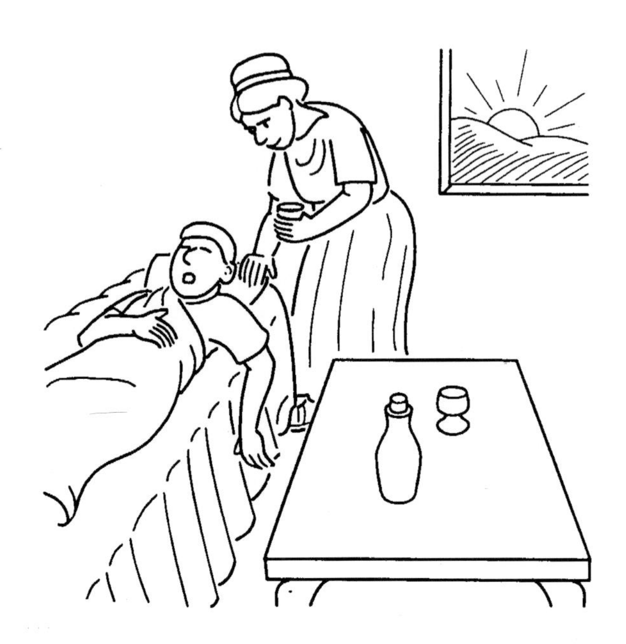

Every culture stretching back through history, so far as we can tell, has known drugs and people who took them for a wide spectrum of reasons: for their healing properties, for insight, or for other mind-altering effects. For example, opium was considered a cure-all in Rome in the second century AD. Cannabis was first used in Europe in 1798 and Queen Victoria was later to take it for period pains. Coca leaves (from which cocaine is produced) have been chewed in South America for centuries to banish tiredness. More recently, Samuel Taylor Coleridge wrote 'Kubla Khan' under opium's influence and Aldous Huxley's 'The Doors of Perception' describes his experience of LSD. Many drugs are naturally occurring (e.g. tobacco, cannabis, khat (see p.22)) or are produced from plant origins (e.g. alcohol, cocaine, heroin) and most were introduced originally for their medical properties by doctors.

What *is* new is the level of availability and scale of use of drugs for non-medical purposes, particularly but not exclusively by young people, and the consequent high profile position that 'drugs' now have in the educational world.

Chapter 1

Setting the Scene

Drugs and young people

This chapter puts the current drugs 'scene' into perspective, drawing a picture which incorporates youthful high jinks and natural curiosity at one end of the scale and the horror stories of addiction and devastation at the other end, whilst also attempting constructively to explore what rests between the two.

The accepted scene

Informed estimates[1] (see p.63) tell us that by the age of 16, as many as half of the youth population will have tried an illegal drug. Though it varies from area to area, this information gives us a useful glimpse of young people today. Even those who have not tried drugs often know someone who has, and where to get them if they ever wanted them. A surprising fact is that they view each other's involvement or otherwise as quite unexceptional. Offers and opportunities abound, wherever one lives in the country, and young people feel free to accept or refuse such offers.[1]

Young people's attitudes to drugs

Howard Parker and Fiona Measham's longitudinal study which has 'followed' over 700 young people in north-west England from 1991 through to 1996 identified four distinct groups. At age 17:

- ✔ 23% were users of one or more illicit drugs (cannabis, amphetamine, LSD)
- ✔ 10% were ex-users who had tried, but didn't expect to use again
- ✔ 36% were abstainers who didn't ever expect to try
- ✔ and the remaining 31% saw themselves as 'in transition': a quarter who had tried and three-quarters who had never tried, but *all* of whom expected to try or use drugs again at some time in the future.

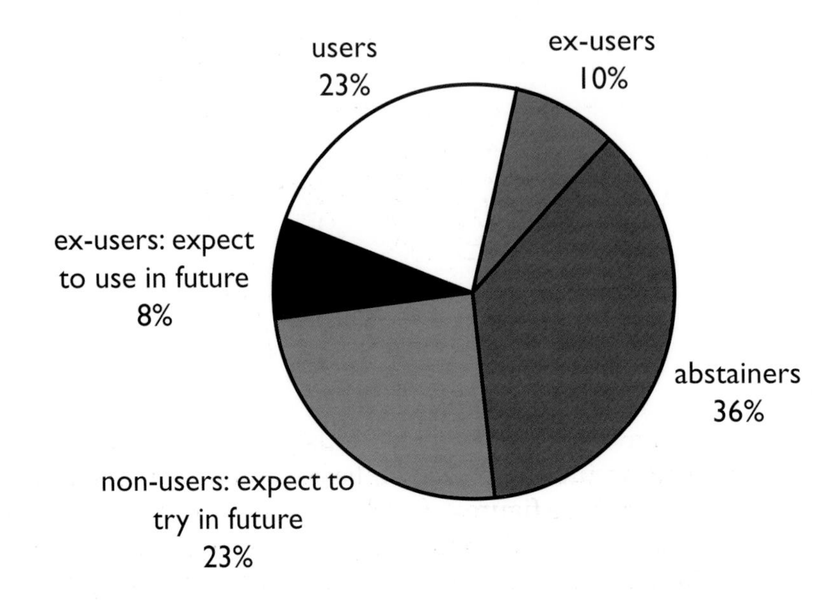

The various groups

Those who say 'yes' mostly do so willingly, and those who want to say 'no' appear to have little difficulty in saying it, and meaning it. The groups, more closely related to personality types than their class origins, are resistant to any intervention encouraging them to change groups. Those who try may be responding to factors such as curiosity, availability, rebellion, temptation, or a wish to court danger or excitement. Drugs are an established part of youth culture.

> *'I've heard it's really amazing, the feeling; I wanna try it!'*
> *'I don't want to miss out.'*
> *'It's just something you do – it's no big deal.'*

Some try and can't seem to get to like it and stop: Parker's 'ex-user' group. Some develop a taste, which often involves a few tries until the whole experience has become familiar and can be planned and steered. They are the huge majority of drug-takers and could be described as occasional or casual users. Their use is generally careful, and enjoyable. The most common drugs taken before the age of 16 are paracetamol, tobacco, alcohol, cannabis, amphetamine, alkyl nitrites and LSD. The most common of the illegal drugs is cannabis resin, crumbled into a hand-rolled cigarette and smoked. Tobacco smoking is usually established before cannabis is tried.

The 'in transition' group say that drugs have some attraction for them, perhaps not much more than 'a good night out' might have for others, but that the possible hassle is not worth it, at least for now. Not for them, the acrimonious relationships at home when they are found out, or the police involvement, or the exclusion from school with exam schedules under threat. They intend to wait until later, when they are at college or in employment and sufficiently independent to be able to use drugs without interference and trouble.

The commonest reason given for using illegal drugs is pleasure. Sometimes there are accidents, which emphasise that drug users may be playing with dangers, but the figures of such accidents do *not* stand out above the statistics of hazards like road accidents, fire, drowning or asthma. Very little drugs use by children leads to death. The following graphs emphasise these points.

Child deaths recorded in a typical year

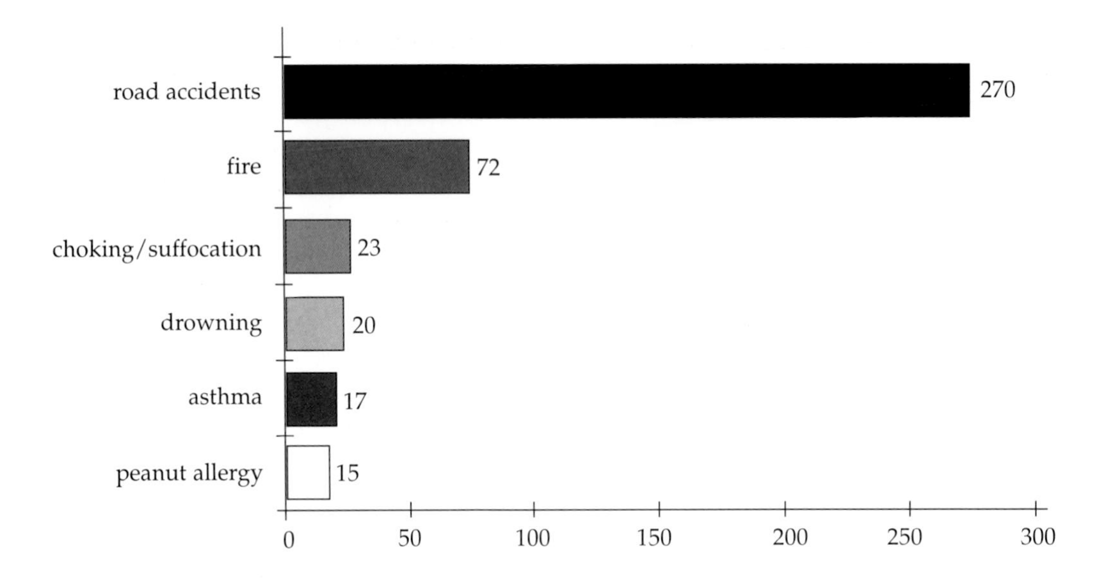

Sources: Department of Toxicology, St George's Hospital, Tooting; Department of the Environment; the Royal Society for the Prevention of Accidents (RoSPA); and The National Asthma Campaign.

Drug deaths (all ages) recorded in a typical year

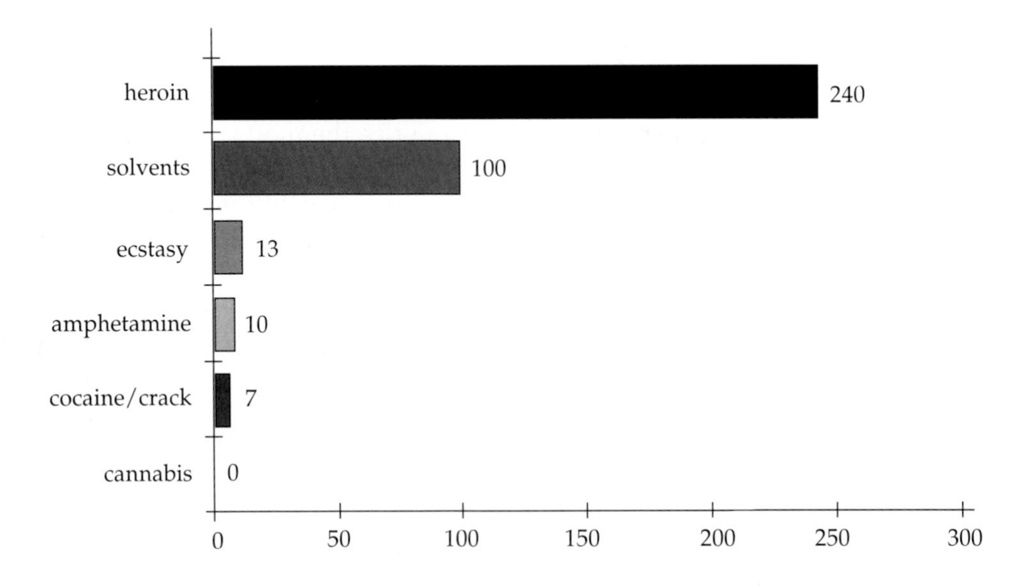

Source: Institute for the Study of Drug Dependence.

Very few of these drug deaths are likely to be children. Using the same scale, the bar for alcohol-related deaths (approximately 30,000 a year, according to *Alcohol Concern*) would be about 33 feet long and the bar for tobacco-related deaths (approximately 110,000 a year, according to *ASH*) would be over 120 feet long.

The need to develop life-skills early

However, quoting statistics does not tell the whole story. The total numbers of people involved in these activities are not comparable: road accidents are not like drug-taking, the proportions of people who have accidents or difficulties vary from pursuit to pursuit, and so on. On the other hand, each of these dreadful statistics represents an individual who was living a life which was probably unexceptional, and facing hazards which are not uncommon. The figures underline a universal need for skill, care, responsibility and a commitment to self-preservation, the development of all of which needs to start in the primary school. Recognition that decisions about drugs require precisely these same attributes shows that drug-taking really isn't intrinsically different from other common, hazardous activities, though society often views it as though it were. It isn't even all illegal – in fact, the legal drugs give rise to many of the worst scenarios overall.

Perhaps the main reason for the fear of illegal drug-taking is the horror stories of lack of control, of ruined lives and of deaths, and though these basic concerns should not be completely subdued, they need to be put into more realistic proportion.

Myths

One reason for fears may be the many drug-related myths and half-truths which masquerade as fact, but which stalwartly refuse to stand up to scrutiny. The press talk of young people being pressured either by their peers or by 'evil' dealers at school gates to the point where they try 'bad' drugs against their will and, by so doing, place themselves on a 'slippery slope' towards chaos and addiction with inevitable subsequent involvement in crime. The true picture is mostly very different from this. In the next few pages, some commonly held myths and half-truths are considered one by one.

Myth 1

'Experimenting is the first step on a slippery slope'

The slope does not appear to be slippery for most drug users. Trying a bit of cannabis and then being curious about amphetamine or nitrites doesn't turn people into criminals or hopeless addicts, though it might get them into trouble. There is also the possibility of accidents due to lack of knowledge or a bad experience.

Those who reach the problematic end of the spectrum of drug use are a small minority, much as alcoholics represent a small proportion of drinkers. A few arrive there through the route of casual drug use, perhaps believing themselves immortal and taking big risks. Others feel able to control their use, and then find they can't, perhaps because of personal pressures or despair. However, the majority of addicts *start* with an unhealthy relationship with drugs.

Problematic use

Almost all have low self-esteem, feel lonely when it matters, have a very bleak view of their futures and have often had other serious personal or social problems for longer than they've been taking drugs. A sizeable minority were sexually abused as children. One not untypical addict put it very graphically when he said:

'My life is so horrible, I have nothing to lose by becoming a junkie.'

Just to be able to make such a statement indicates a pretty negative state of mind, and an unenviable set of personal circumstances. Problematic use doesn't happen by chance, it is generally one of a combination of interrelated factors.

A close parallel to illustrate this is involvement with alcohol. Most people drink it, at least on some occasions. Those who don't include some who tried it and didn't like it or its effects. Those who do like it use it predominantly in social situations for enjoyment.

Alcohol is a powerful and addictive drug, yet it is a very small proportion of drinkers who become alcoholics. A look at alcoholics shows a group of people who almost always have other serious problems in their lives, which in many cases were there before the alcoholism. They don't drink for enjoyment and often drink alone. This pattern of use sets them apart from other alcohol users. 'Social' drinkers have proved that regular use of alcohol does not, by itself, make alcoholism more likely, as is also the case with other non-medicinal drugs.

Addiction isn't automatic, even with heroin or 'crack'. It has to be worked for and tends to accompany a range of other individual, personal and social ills which often combine to make drug-taking a more attractive heavy-duty option than it ever is for most users. A salutary and reassuring fact is that most users of illegal drugs do so for fun and experience few problems. For those who do experience long-term problems like addiction, disruption to relationships, or chaotic lifestyle, the devastation can be as great whether the drug is legal or illegal.

The 'slippery slope' therefore is largely mythical.

Myth 2

'Drug-taking leads to crime'

Most illegal drug-taking is casual and is paid for from legitimate disposable income (pocket money, Saturday job, full employment, Social Security benefits, and so on). It may be cheaper than an evening at the pub. Disproportionately large amounts of acquisitive crime are committed by a relatively small number of people, who may use drugs in a dependent way, but also buy alcohol, food, rent, bus fares, petrol, cigarettes ... . Their activity is never called 'rent-related crime'. Their thieving often has earlier roots than their drug use, or else the two activities are likely to have grown up side by side, neither causing the other. The relationship between the two activities is often considered a simple cause-and-effect one; in fact, like all social issues, any such relationship is complex. Drug-taking *can* directly lead to crime, but for the majority, it doesn't.

Myth 3

'Drug-laced tattoos are being offered to primary school children'

Duplicated information sheets, sometimes claiming to have come from the police, have been circulating since the 1980s, warning parents and teachers about 'Blue Star Triangles' and 'transfers with cartoon motifs laced with LSD and strychnine'. This is a well-documented[2] (see p.63) urban myth. These 'tattoos' do not and never have existed. Though LSD is often supplied impregnated into small pieces of paper, the chances of these getting into the hands of small children is no greater than with any other drug.

Myth 4

'Impurities are more dangerous than the drugs they are mixed with'

This is possible, but rare and may be devastating if it does occur. Analysis of actual samples of street drugs, including those that are illicitly produced and smuggled into the country, reveals a range of impurities, often there as a result of the manufacturing process rather than added later, and only sometimes having psycho-active or mood-altering properties. For example, caffeine and ketamine (see p.22) have been found masquerading as ecstasy. Street heroin still contains many of the constituents of the original opium as well as bulking agents such as caffeine or lactose. Psycho-active impurities can increase danger by adding to unpredictability. Though powdered glass, battery acid and brick dust sometimes appear in warnings aimed at young people, they don't appear in analyses. Greater danger is often represented by an unusually pure sample leading to possible overdose due to users taking more of the substance than they realise.

Myth 5

'You can't get addicted if you don't inject'

This is untrue. If the drug is physically addictive, addiction is always possible from repeated doses. With all drugs, including solvents, alkyl nitrites, cannabis and amphetamine which are not physically addictive, a psychological dependence is possible. Such emotional attachment to drug-taking may represent a stronger bond than a purely physical one, whatever the drug. Some injecting users seem to be strongly dependent upon the act of injecting and the ritual this process involves.

Myth 6

'Cannabis is harmless'

Physical damage, even after long periods of use, is hard to detect and none has been conclusively proved despite the efforts of many to demonstrate it. However, the damage that chaotic cannabis use can do to lifestyle, relationships, reliability and prospects, for example, is unquestionable. Heavy users may redirect time and money to securing a supply; concentration and short-term memory may be disrupted, and so on. Much will depend upon the reason for use, the scale of involvement and the other significant personal circumstances of the user. The potential for harm from cannabis has often been grossly exaggerated, often because of the wrong assumption that it inevitably 'leads on to other drugs', but it should not be described as harmless.

Myth 7

'Supplies to our children are likely to start with a dealer at the primary school gates'

A dealer wanting to establish a reliable market does not usually go to one of the most visible sites imaginable and attempt to recruit unreliable people of severely restricted financial means. It has been known at secondary schools, though not usually for long! If you ever see anything that answers this description, tell the police at once and let them take prompt and appropriate action.

The commonest source of drugs is someone known to the buyer, often a friend. Networks of supply are now enormous and many small-time users buy a little more than they need and sell it on to help to pay for their supply. Others are the buyers for more than one person, sometimes each member of a group of friends taking turns to 'score' for the others. Whereas the letter of the law makes little distinction between one small-scale dealer and another (supplying controlled drugs is a serious crime – an important point for young people to realise), we need to be aware that contact between 'professional' dealers whose principal or sole source of income is from their dealing, and school-age children is not common, unless the dealers are their parents.

Myth 8

'Drugs are bad'

If all drugs were bad, the label would have to include alcohol, tobacco, caffeine and paracetamol. Heroin is used in hospitals. Alcohol kills people – a similar number of children *first time* as are killed by ecstasy – and across all ages the annual figure is between 28,000 and 33,000. Paracetamol kills, cannabis doesn't. The more one tries to define exactly what makes a drug bad, the more other drugs slip unwanted into the same definitions. It is much more useful to think of drugs as like cars. Both are inanimate, both can kill, though neither is inherently 'bad'. With cars, our most useful principal focus is the driver. Do they have a licence? Do they understand the dangers? Are they familiar with the car and the route? What is the weather like? Have they been drinking? With drugs, our main concern should also be the person, the pupil, and all the work we can do to ensure that all relevant issues are addressed, appropriately and in their proper place – responsibility, health and safety, rules and laws, excitement and risk, relationships, decision-making, and so on. Every drug, like every car, represents potential danger but none harms without human involvement.

Myth 9

'Ecstasy is safe for all but an unlucky few'

We don't yet fully understand the dangers of ecstasy. Some seem to have an acute idiosyncratic reaction to the drug. For those who tragically died through drinking too much water, or through a combination of dehydration and raised body temperature, it wasn't bad luck, it was ignorance, bad judgement, or both. We are largely in the dark about long-term dangers, although it is unhelpful to assume that any long-term effects of use are necessarily bad. If there are any, they may turn out not to be significant. We don't know, and we oughtn't to pretend we do. On the other hand, there is a large group of people out there, conducting a long-term experiment as guinea pigs. They are taking a chance.

Myth 10

'The best drugs education strategy is to teach children to resist peer pressure'

This statement is founded upon a mistaken belief that peer pressure is commonly a significant reason for trying drugs. Some work has been done by Niall Coggans and Susan McKellar[3] (see p.63) addressing the term 'peer pressure', and casting doubt upon its role as a factor in young people's experimentation with drugs. They point out that young people make friendship groups which include others with similar tastes, ideas and attitudes. So risk-takers may band together, as may rebels, chess-players, computer game *aficionados*, supporters of the same football team or avid fans of the same film star. One group may naturally shy away from drugs, however often they are on offer. However, another set of young friends may, *as a group*, feel more readily inclined towards trying drugs, and if so, it is likely that all the members in such a group will find them attractive, precisely because peer groups tend to share beliefs, values and behaviours. They don't need to pressure each other. It is probably because they share similar outlooks that they formed a bond in the first place.

Coggans and McKellar suggest that the peer group may constitute a supportive place to go *after the decision to try drugs has been made,* in order to find social approval for this behaviour. They cite much research and careful analysis of the evidence, and conclude that, although there is undoubtedly influence upon the individuals within groups, early socialising factors are more likely to determine attitude to drugs than peer pressure. This understanding has been powerful in influencing current approaches to drugs education. Educational strategies which are more useful than a focus upon resisting peer pressure are dealt with in later chapters.

Chapter 2

The need to educate

Human nature

It would be unhelpful to dismiss drug-taking as mere deviant behaviour, with something 'wrong' with the people who do it. A more caring alternative view, namely that the drugs are somehow evil, with the power to enslave children and steal them away from good and productive ways of life, may have spawned the expression 'the war on drugs', but there is a need to ensure that such a war is not transmuted in practice into a war on young people, for children need our help. It can be tempting, if one subscribes to the 'children are good, drugs are bad' view, to believe that drugs education should attempt to keep the two apart. However, a more realistic role for drugs education is to help young people to grow up safely in a world not of their making, where drugs are far more accessible than they were when we were young. In order for such a task to be addressed in an effective and sensitive way, we need to try to understand what makes some people try drugs in the first place.

Curiosity

Curiosity is a significant factor. It is one of the things that make small children tick. A sense of adventure, a wish to discover the world and their place in it, enjoyment of the forbidden and a belief in their immortality all contribute to a range of worrying behaviours. Running across the road, climbing trees, jumping off bridges into rivers, riding bikes with no lights at night are just a few examples. When we were young, some children who did naughty things – smoking behind the bushes, stealing sweets from the corner shop, throwing conkers at passing cars – were simply experimenting with whatever exciting activities were available. That's often what young people who try drugs are doing.

Following examples

Another significant factor is the example set by adults. Many reach rather too easily for headache tablets, or tranquillisers, or a glass of wine at the end of the day to help them unwind. In so doing, they may set a powerful example to children that there is a chemical answer ready for whenever they don't feel quite OK, and that it is fine to use these chemicals, even when they are not ill, to make them *feel different*.

It may well be for these reasons that many young people think it is acceptable to try drugs. Their eyes grow wide when parents or teachers hit the roof with anger or worry because the drugs they try are not the ones adults use and they smell double standards. Copying, inquisitiveness, the natural rebellion of the growing adolescent and a readiness to take risks is an extremely potent combination. Young people have had all these characteristics since time began.

Accepted behaviour

It is even harder to describe drug-taking as deviant now that we are probably fast approaching the time when over half of the 16 year-olds in the UK will have tried an illegal drug. Any wish to 'stem the tide' may be impossible to fulfil. Young people (largely) have taken casual drug use into their culture in a way that we need to try to understand. For them, it is not surprising or out of the ordinary behaviour whether they are themselves involved or not. Abstainers do not generally throw up their hands in horror at those who use drugs. They shrug their shoulders and do their own thing.

Young people naturally wish to be closely involved with what is considered hip, groovy or cool for the new millennium. The involvement of drugs in this picture may be surprising or regrettable, but it is undeniable. Perversely, drug use to a teenager may at times be no more and no less than a fashion statement. Knowing this makes it even more important to start exploring the issues responsibly, as early as we can.

Protecting children's safety

We need to protect the youngest children, reminding them when necessary that the world can be a dangerous place to live, and helping them to develop the skills and the will to protect themselves. Whatever our views about drugs and those who use them, while even small numbers of young people are dying, there is still more effective work for us to do.

There are three main causes of serious problems with drugs – accident, ignorance and recklessness.

Accidents

There will always be accidents. With road safety, we try to increase the skills and awareness of pupils, help them to understand and practise safety rules and alert them to dangers. Our intention is not to alarm them, still less to make them rigid with fear, but to ensure that they are well informed and ready to take proper responsibility for their own welfare.

However, of 44,835 road accidents involving children aged 0–15 in Great Britain in 1996, 82% were on built-up roads and 42% of the children injured or killed were pedestrians. 270 children died. Two-thirds were boys. There is no public panic about these figures, nor would it help if there were. We just have to keep trying to help children to avoid accidents the best way we know how, by teaching them, talking to them, letting them know how important each of them is, and reminding adults to drive more slowly. Though drug use is different, precisely the same educational principles apply.

Ignorance

Ignorance is much easier to banish. We include the information young people need in our teaching programmes, and ensure that it is accurate, relevant and credible.

Recklessness

Recklessness can take either of two forms – bravado or self-destruction. Bravado can be linked to a feeling of immortality, a wish for attention, status and recognition, or bad judgement placing personal safety below the wish for excitement and gratification. Self-destructive behaviour is usually related to a belief in personal unworthiness, leading to a general lack of concern for safety. Its manifestation is not confined to drug users and the strategy for addressing it is the same in any case – raise and maintain self-esteem and aid its self-maintenance. People with high self-esteem are considerably less likely to court death, as long as they know where the dangers lie, and are also far less likely ever to become problematic drug users, whatever they may try for fun.

Why start so young?

Drugs are here to stay, young people cannot be shielded from contact with them or from hearing about them and the process of ensuring the skills are there to cope in such a world is a slow one which takes time.

Do we threaten their innocence?

Many people speak of the innocence of children being threatened by introduction too early to a range of unpalatable realities. It seems very regrettable that we have to lock doors where we used not to, that we fear sexual attacks by predatory perverts, that children can no longer roam the countryside freely on bicycles on hot summer days without driving parents sick with worry until they return safely. Many schools now have ID cards to be signed for on entry, to ensure proper security. To the extent that the world has changed, rather than our level of consciousness of how it has always been, it is very sad.

Whether it is right to consider pupils 'innocent' about drugs can be tested. The Draw and Write technique[4] (see p.63), developed by Noreen Wetton, has helped us to realise that even infant school children know more than we realise about drugs. They hear their parents and older siblings talking, they talk to each other in the playground, they watch teenage 'soaps' and the early evening news. They read the papers, encouraged by teachers! By junior school age, they often have quite a sophisticated level of drugs awareness, frequently not matched by accuracy or understanding. They show themselves to be neither ignorant nor innocent, and may have quite urgent need for sound and caring input in order to challenge myths, scotch rumours and correct misunderstandings.

The Draw and Write technique is very useful for helping to determine the appropriate starting points. It is described in more detail on pp.36–37.

What are their needs?

Even young children have needs to understand drugs and medicines. Schools should find out what these needs are and meet them professionally, sensitively and responsibly. The children themselves, their lifestyles and their experiences should lead you, together with their own questions and concerns, rather than educational theories or your fears. If they are not yet ready for information or a skill, wait. You can find out their level of need by determining their current level of understanding – they will usually be happy to tell you what they know if you ask them.

Do we stimulate curiosity?

Another fear which is routinely voiced by the teachers is that, by raising issues, we may stimulate curiosity. This may be true if the subject is raised in inappropriate ways, bringing information to children for which they are not ready and have no need. There is official, detailed guidance about the possible content of drugs education at all stages of education, but it should never override the judgement of the class teacher. Only you know what you have already talked about with them on this subject and you know them better than authors or politicians. You will know if a question is put as a provocation or is born of genuine curiosity. If you judge that a particular explanation is not appropriate now, or not suitable for the whole class, then be guided by that.

However, you *may* stimulate curiosity unavoidably but it is better that *you* talk to your pupils than someone 'out there' with no thought for their readiness or their needs. In the early years, the caring approach you can bring may be just what is needed to temper a child's adventurous curiosity and feelings of immortality with common sense and the need for natural caution. You can also make it legitimate to talk about the subject, setting the scene for vital secondary school work. To nurture openness may be highly significant if, in the longer run, someone in great need feels brave enough to talk about what is happening to them, and how they are feeling about it.

Developing their social skills

The final reason for starting drugs education at the age of five or six stems from the fact that drugs are not tried in isolation from other people. Usually it is a social event – a group all having fun together – and there may be some safety in the very numbers. Offers of drugs, and acceptances, are between people. The skills to deal with relationships are consequently as important in drugs education as they are in any other element of Personal, Social and Health Education. With drugs as one among many PSHE topics, elements common to all, such as social skills acquisition and practice, relationship making and breaking, dealing constructively with conflict, using information to support decision-making, should be addressed progressively with the development of the individual. In order to be given adequate attention, this process must start early in the child's school career and take a steady, low-profile but continual part in the curriculum.

The National Healthy School Standard launched in Autumn 1999 has been designed to support and complement the new PSHE framework in schools in England across all four Key Stages. It acknowledges the role of primary schools is an important one in laying the foundations of lasting good health.

Chapter 3

The more well-known drugs

The laws relating to drugs

As pupils progress from age five to eleven, they will need to have a slowly growing realisation that some drugs are restricted and some are not, that there are laws which lay down these restrictions, and in most cases good reasons for them. The overall picture is that some drugs are entirely legal (e.g. caffeine, ketamine); for some, the supply and/or use are controlled (e.g. tobacco, alcohol, 'over-the-counter' medicines); some should only be possessed with a doctor's prescription (e.g. tranquillisers, barbiturates); some are normally only used legally by a doctor (e.g. heroin); and some are forbidden under any circumstances (e.g. ecstasy). There is no requirement to provide primary school pupils with the fine detail of the law but some information about laws may be of use as the subject of drugs is progressively raised and explored. Introduction to these laws is advised in the SCAA/DfEE guidance documents to begin at Key Stage 2. A good starting point is often the rules governing behaviour at home and at school, recommended at Key Stage 1. A summary of the principal drug laws follows. These apply throughout the UK unless otherwise stated.

The Misuse of Drugs Act 1971

	Class A	Class B	Class C
Drugs included	opium, heroin, methadone, cocaine, crack, LSD, ecstasy, processed 'magic' mushrooms, any Class B drug prepared for injection	amphetamines, cannabis resin, 'herbal' cannabis and hash oil, barbiturates, codeine	mild amphetamines, tranquillisers, DF 118 (painkillers), (most) anabolic steroids
Maximum penalties for possession	7 years + a fine	5 years + a fine	2 years + a fine
Maximum penalties for trafficking	Life imprisonment + a fine	14 years + a fine	5 years + a fine

These are the maximum penalties a Crown Court can impose. A magistrate is restricted to imposing a maximum of 6 months' imprisonment and a fine of £2,000. It is important to realise that these maximum sentences will depend upon previous offences and other factors. They are not automatic. Minimum penalties are much less. Police have the power to caution and not prosecute in some situations.

Alcohol – subject to Licensing Regulations

It is illegal to *supply* anyone with alcohol under the age of five. After that, the law is concerned principally with how alcohol is obtained and where it is consumed. So, legally speaking, a six year-old may drink alcohol, though not on licensed premises. *Purchase* of beer, cider, perry (and, in Scotland, wine) are permitted at age 14 in licensed restaurants to drink with a meal (except Northern Ireland). *Purchase* of all alcohol from licensed premises (pub, off-licence) is permitted from age 18. *Sale* of alcohol to under 18s is forbidden on these premises. *Possession* is an offence on some trains or coaches to designated sporting events. Suppliers of alcohol, such as those supervising supermarket checkouts, must be over 18. *Consumption* may not take place on off-licence premises, nor in some city centres with such bye-laws. It is an offence to be *drunk* in a public place and in pubs, or to drive while unfit, that is currently with more than 80 mg of alcohol in 100 ml of blood. Since the summer of 1997, the Confiscation of Alcohol (Young Persons) Act 1997 has permitted police to confiscate alcohol in public places from people under the age of 18.

Tobacco

The *possession* and *use* of tobacco are unrestricted, although police officers and park keepers have the authority to confiscate tobacco from children under the age of 16. (Schools will have their own internal rules!) The *sale* of tobacco to persons under the age of 16 is illegal.

Solvents

The *possession* and *use* of solvents are unrestricted, although in some areas bye-laws allow police to take sniffers in public to 'a place of safety'. In Scotland, they can be taken into care. The Intoxicating Substances Supply Act 1985 operates in England, Wales and Northern Ireland to restrict retailers from *supplying* solvents to anyone under 18 if they have reason to believe they will be used for purposes of intoxication. Scotland has broadly similar arrangements under common law. Since October 1999, the Consumer Protection Act has made it illegal in the UK to sell butane to under 18s in any circumstances.

Medicines

Medicines are controlled by the Medicines Agency, which regulates the manufacture and supply of medicines through licensed outlets: chemists, corner shops and so on. Possession of some medicines (e.g. temazepam) which are prescription-only is illegal under the Misuse of Drugs Act if no prescription is held. Other prescription-only medicines (e.g. ketamine) are not controlled in this way.

Drugs: a short guide

This chapter contains a short, quick-reference guide to the drugs most likely to be under discussion in primary school classes, such as alcohol, amphetamines, cannabis, paracetamol, solvents and tobacco. This is a somewhat subjective choice, but is an attempt to provide an easily digestible section, principally for teacher reference. A fuller guide is included as an appendix (pp.55–60).

Neither this section nor the full guide is intended to be a comprehensive source of information about the drugs included in it. The drugs less commonly to be found, almost never used by children even of secondary school age, and consequently a lesser source of anxiety for the primary teacher, such as heroin, cocaine, GHB, khat, ketamine and barbiturates, are not included at all in the guides. Teachers wishing to learn about the effects of these and other drugs should refer to a reliable and reputable source such as ISDD's excellent guide, *Drug Abuse Briefing*.

Drug name	**Alcohol**
Chemical name *(if applicable)*	Ethyl alcohol
Variants	Occurs in various types of alcoholic drink, e.g. wine, spirits, beers, ciders
Brand names	Too many to list
Slang names	Booze, bevvy, drink
Group	Depressants
Status	Legal, subject to age and consumption restraints.
Short term	A unit of alcohol lasts for about 1 hour. Loss of inhibition, light-headedness, relaxation. Progressive doses impair judgement, balance, co-ordination.
Dangers	Effects are more powerful on smaller people and those with low tolerance. Lack of control and judgement impair skills such as driving and operating machinery. Possible addiction.

Drug name	**Alkyl nitrites**
Chemical name *(if applicable)*	Amyl nitrite, butyl nitrite, iso-butyl nitrite
Variants	Amyl nitrite is a medicine. Others sold in sex shops, etc.
Brand names	Locker Room, KIX, Rock Hard
Slang names	Poppers, liquid gold, stud, rush, room freshener
Group	Stimulants
Status	Possession is legal.
Short term	A strong stimulant, usually inhaled from soaked material. A euphoric rush is almost immediate but short-lived. Nausea, cold sweats, dermatitis less frequent.
Dangers	People with heart trouble, anaemia or glaucoma should avoid nitrites. Excessive use is hazardous.

Drug name	**Amphetamines**
Chemical name *(if applicable)*	Amphetamine sulphate
Variants	Slimming pills, pharmaceutical preparations, illegal powders and pills
Brand names	Dexedrine, Ritalin, Tenuate Dospan, etc.
Slang names	Speed, whizz, uppers, Billy, sulphate
Group	Stimulants
Status	Prescription only, otherwise illegal, Class B.
Short term	Effects last 3–4 hours. Users feel more energetic and powerful. Suppresses appetite. Restlessness and anxiety, exhaustion and hunger may follow. Takes a day or more to recover.
Dangers	Injection. Not meeting body's need for rest and nourishment.

Drug name	**Paracetamol**
Variants	Over-the-counter pain-killing preparations and cold remedies
Brand names	Paracetamol, Calpol, Lem-Sip, etc.
Slang names	'Headache tablets', etc.
Group	Analgesic
Status	Legal medicine, may be purchased from pharmacies without prescription.
Short term	Dulls pain effectively for periods of up to 4 hours.
Dangers	Accidental deaths recorded every year from overdose, often boosting dose by combining products. 15 tablets may be an overdose for an adult, less for children.

Drug name	**Caffeine**
Chemical name *(if applicable)*	Caffeine. Since 1904, it has replaced cocaine as an ingredient in Coca-Cola.
Variants	In chocolate, and coffee, tea and cola drinks unless decaffeinated
Brand names	Nescafé, PG Tips, Pepsi-Cola, Pro-Plus, Herbal Booster, etc.
Slang names	None
Group	Stimulants
Status	Legal, 70% of adults drink coffee and 86% drink tea (in the UK), Pro-Plus tablets available without prescription from pharmacies.
Short term	Caffeine stimulates the nervous system. Users feel awake and alert, reducing boredom and tiredness. Larger doses reduce co-ordination and increase heart rate and blood pressure. It is a diuretic. When effects wear off, user may feel more tired.
Dangers	7–10 cups of strong tea/coffee a day can cause chronic anxiety, irritability, headache and chronic insomnia. Missed dose, particularly early morning, can cause tiredness and irritability.

Drug name	**Cannabis**
Chemical name *(if applicable)*	Cannabinoids, from the Cannabis Sativa plant
Variants	Hashish, marijuana; dried leaves/seeds or resin in blocks
Brand names	None
Slang names	Blow, dope, draw, ganja, grass, hash, puff, resin, spliff, skunk, etc.
Group	Hallucinogens
Status	Illegal. Class B.
Short term	Effects – relaxation, and a state of well-being and heightened senses – start quickly and last an hour or so. Giggling, hunger, short-term memory loss and confusion also possible.
Dangers	Chronic use may lead to general apathy. May aggravate mental illness. Co-ordination impaired. Discovery by those in authority.

Drug name	**Solvents** (commonly used name for volatile substances)
Chemical name *(if applicable)*	Toluene, acetone, fluorocarbons (propellants from aerosols), petrol, trichloroethane, etc.
Variants	Any volatile substance giving off a heavy vapour, gases, fuels
Brand names	Ronson lighter fuel, Evo-Stik, Camping Gaz, Shell 4-star, etc.
Slang names	Sniff
Group	Depressants
Status	Legal, supply restricted in some circumstances to under 18s.
Short term	Very similar effects to alcohol, but shorter lived. Vapour sniffed from bag, canister, soaked material causes intoxication and stupor. High spirits and impaired co-ordination, judgement. Recovery usually quick, even from unconsciousness.
Dangers	Asphyxia from bag covering face or inhaled vomit. Freezing of airways following sniffing direct from pressurised container.

Drug name	**Tobacco**
Chemical name *(if applicable)*	Nicotine, principally in tobacco
Variants	Cigarettes, pipe and rolling tobacco, cigars, nicotine patches
Brand names	No 6, Hamlet, Old Holborn, Three Nuns, Nicorette, etc.
Slang names	Ciggies, fags, smokes, roll-ups, cancer sticks, etc.
Group	Stimulants
Status	Legal to possess and smoke at any age, licensed suppliers may not sell to under 16s.
Short term	Absorbed into bloodstream via inhaled smoke. Increases heart rate and blood pressure, stimulates and arouses the nervous system. Addictive, with unpleasant withdrawal symptoms.
Dangers	Premature death from active or passive smoking. Causes respiratory disorders; increased risk from oral contraceptives.

Chapter

4

From theory to practice

Official guidance documents

Some of the following documents do not apply everywhere in Britain. In Scotland, there is no National Curriculum and pupils are not grouped by key stage. The Scottish and Welsh Offices ensure that local references are included in their versions of documents even where they have similar titles to those applying elsewhere, and curriculum guidance depends on local policy as well as the legislative framework. The language describing the documents listed in the book will usually indicate where they are valid, where this is not made explicit.

A. Documents for schools in England and Wales

Aside from local LEA or Health Authority guidance, there is a group of important documents providing schools with helpful information about the structure and delivery of drugs education, and the options facing schools responding to incidents involving drugs.

1. **Section 351 of the Education Act 1996** requires that 'The curriculum for a school satisfies the requirements of this section if it is a balanced and broadly based curriculum which:

   a) promotes the spiritual, moral, cultural, mental and physical development of pupils at the school and of society; and
   b) prepares pupils at the school for the opportunities, responsibilities and experiences of adult life.'

2. **Curriculum Guidance 3: The Whole Curriculum**, National Curriculum Council (NCC), 1990
   This document is still current, relevant and in many schools, though out of print. It emphasises the importance of the spirit and ethos of the school, its pupils and its staff, and pinpoints personal and social skills and effective teaching methods as of particular significance. It also asserts that the education system has 'a duty to educate individuals to be able to think and act for themselves'.

3. **Curriculum Guidance 5: Health Education,** NCC, 1990
   This useful booklet (also current but out of print) offers generic Health Education guidance. It encourages schools to develop a Health Education policy and it cites 'Substance Use and Misuse' as one of nine components of Health Education, suggesting appropriate areas of study for all nine, at each key stage in England and Wales.

4. **Circular 4/95: Drug Prevention and Schools**, DfEE, 1995
   This circular gives detailed guidance as to the role of schools in relation to curriculum input and response to incidents and was circulated to all schools in England and Wales.

5. **Drug Education: Curriculum Guidance for Schools,** Schools Curriculum and Assessment Authority (SCAA), 1995
   This essential guidance document supports the planning and organisation of drugs education with reference to timetabling, content and Health Education principles. It provides detailed suggestions about the knowledge, skills and attitudes that need to be addressed at each key stage in England and Wales.

6. **Drug Education in Schools**, OFSTED, 1997
   This report describes recent progress in practice based on a detailed survey through questionnaire and analysis of school visits and inspections in England.

7. **Protecting Young People: Good Practice in Drug Education in Schools and the Youth Service**, DfEE, 1998
   This document augments previous guidance in the light of experience. It follows publication of the White Paper 'Tackling Drugs to Build a Better Britain' (described on p.28) and supplements advice given in the DfEE Circular 4/95 on drugs education and managing incidents. The document can be accessed at the following internet address: http://www.dfee.gov.co.uk/protect/index.htm

8. **A Framework for Personal, Social and Health Education and Citizenship at Key Stages 1–4**
   In the guidelines for PSHE and Citizenship in the National Curriculum (with effect from September 2000), there are numerous elements at Key Stages 1 and 2 which relate directly or indirectly to drugs. For instance, the guidelines say pupils should learn the basic rules and skills for keeping themselves healthy and safe and for managing their behaviour, as they begin to take some responsibility for themselves. Schools are also encouraged to teach pupils the skills, knowledge and understanding they will need to develop a healthy lifestyle and keep themselves and others safe, to ask for help when they need it, but also to begin to take responsiblilty for finding for themselves the information and advice they need. (See also page 33.)

B. Documents for schools in England, Wales and Scotland

9. **HM Government White Paper 'Tackling Drugs to Build a Better Britain'**, HMSO, 1998
The White Paper sets out the government's ten-year strategy for tackling drugs issues. Guidance Notes published at the same time were aimed at those with responsibility for implementing the strategy. Of particular relevance to schools are pp.13–16 in the White Paper and pp.11–15 in the Guidance Notes. The full strategy can be accessed at the following internet address:
http://www.official-documents.co.uk/document/cm39/3945/3945.htm

10. **The Right Choice: Guidance on Selecting Drug Education Materials for Schools**, SCODA/DEF, 1998
This is a very helpful 28-page booklet providing a wealth of concise help in assessing and choosing the best drugs education materials for the task.

11. **The Right Approach: Quality Standards in Drug Education**, SCODA, 1999
This details a list of quality standards against which drugs education provision may be assessed.

12. **The Right Responses: Managing and Making Policy for Drug-related Incidents in Schools**, SCODA, 1999
This guides schools in setting effective and realistic drugs policy and managing any drug-related incidents or situations which arise at school.

C. Documents for schools in Scotland

13. **The Scottish Office document *The Structure and Balance of the Curriculum*** states among the aims of education 5–14:

'• understanding and appreciation of themselves and other people and of the world about them
• the capacity for independent thought through enquiry, problem solving, information handling and reasoning
• appreciation of the benefits of healthy living and physical fitness.'

It also says:
'The curriculum should help them to identify and reflect on the values which they and society hold and should contribute positively to the understanding of rules, rights and responsibilities, to the ability to distinguish right from wrong, and to an appreciation of good behaviour, courtesy and respect for others.'

14. **Drug Education Approaches, Effectiveness and Implications for Delivery**, Health Education Board for Scotland, 1995
ISBN 1 873452 75 6
This HEBS Working Paper No 1 was written by Niall Coggans and Jonathan Watson and identifies realistic approaches to drugs education. It may also be available from Health Promotion Department resource libraries.

15. **Issues in Health Education and Health Promotion**, Scottish Office and Education and Industry Department, 1996
This is an HMI report.

16. **Drugs in Scotland: Meeting the Challenge**, HMSO, 1996
This report is from the Ministerial Drugs Task Force.

17. The Heart of the Matter, Scottish CCC, 1995
This short booklet contains a sensitive and thoughtful discussion of 'education for personal development'.

18. Guidelines for the Management of Drug Misuse in Schools, Scottish Executive, 1999
Draft guidance produced by the School Drug Safety Team.

The principles of drugs education

When education about drugs was first widened to include illegal drugs, it often took the form of one-off lessons to upper secondary school pupils, concentrating on danger. However, the numbers who try illegal drugs have continued to rise steadily, requiring reconsideration of how and when to teach about drugs.

Older pupils have told researchers that they do not appreciate exaggerated warnings or attempts to make their decisions for them but that they greatly value honesty and accurate, reliable information. They want a chance to be heard, and for education to give them the skills and understanding they will need to make decisions about drugs. The skill to be assertive in the face of persuasion is certainly important to acquire, but because almost all young people who experiment with drugs do so because they want to, the relevance this skill has to drug-related situations is limited.

It is becoming generally accepted that teachers must use strategies which work *with* young people rather than *against* them.

The Draw and Write technique (see pp.36–37) tells us unequivocally that drugs education needs to begin at age five.

At primary level

The principles of primary school drugs education can be clearly set out:

✔ **Drugs education needs to start from where children are and appeal to their integrity.**
Starting points should be gleaned from the pupils themselves, using the Draw and Write technique mentioned above, and the approach should convey trust that the pupils will develop the competence they need.

✔ **Drugs education needs to start early and be revisited continually in the early years.**
Saying things once only is neither appropriate nor sufficient. Skills need to be practised, situations talked about, options considered. To re-examine issues can extend children's comprehension as their experience grows and their horizons broaden.

✔ **Drugs education needs to take an unobtrusive place in more general PSHE.**
Drugs education is not an isolated 'subject'. The skills and self-knowledge it encourages are widely applicable. It needs to be set sensitively in the context of references to life and lives with which young people can identify.

✔ **The skills needed to teach about drugs are the same skills required for addressing any element of PSHE.**
Drugs education does not require unique skills. Teachers need to be able to facilitate discussion, listen carefully, remain impartial when appropriate, use approaches which are non-threatening and which involve pupils actively, and to know their pupils' needs.

✔ **Teachers who know their pupils well are ideally placed to provide sensitive drugs education.**
Primary school teachers frequently have a class long enough to know their pupils' personalities really well. They can judge when they are ready for ideas or information, whether questions are genuine or merely provocative and can temper their input accordingly. This is always much harder for visitors.

✔ **Teachers don't need to be drugs experts to teach about the subject.**
The expertise that is vital is knowing the children and using relevant teaching styles. Information can always be found in suitable reference material.

✔ **A focus upon exploring attitudes and values, and developing and practising skills is likely to be more beneficial than dependence upon information-giving.**
Young minds often need to have early ideas challenged in ways which do not demean or otherwise discourage openness. Pupils may assume their peers concur with their views. Activities which encourage many opinions can test such assumptions and ensure that each pupil receives 'input' from many sources, not just the teacher. 'Drug facts' form only a small part of drugs education.

✔ **Approaches which are interactive and facilitative are more effective in gaining co-operation and making lasting changes.**
If the pupils are active and not mere recipients, their learning is likely to be deeper, more personal and longer-lasting.

The aims of drugs education

It is necessary for each school to set aims for the drugs education it provides, in order to ensure clarity and unison. Without such aims, there could be confusion and disparity. Your school is more likely to reach its aims if they are explicit. Beware of setting yourselves unrealistic goals, such as 'to stop our pupils trying drugs', which may be beyond your power to reach.

A useful starting point is the overarching aim stated in the SCAA guidance document:

> 'The purpose should be to give young people the knowledge, skills and attitudes to appreciate the benefits of a healthy lifestyle and relate these to their own actions, both now and in their future lives.'

However, more detailed aims have not been laid down, and schools must therefore specify their own if everyone is to be clear about what the school is setting out to achieve. I would suggest that you use the following set of aims as a framework for your school:

Suggested aims

- ✔ To help our pupils to recognise that each is unique, valuable and irreplaceable.
- ✔ To help our pupils to maintain their own and each other's self-esteem.
- ✔ To create a climate in which our pupils feel comfortable discussing their perceptions of drugs.
- ✔ To use principally active learning techniques.
- ✔ To help our pupils to develop their knowledge and understanding of medicines and other drugs and how they are used.
- ✔ To provide a range of activities and opportunities for learning about drugs and the issues raised by their use.
- ✔ To help our pupils to develop their knowledge and understanding of themselves.
- ✔ To develop our pupils' decision-making skills.
- ✔ To present opportunities for our pupils to explore their feelings, attitudes and needs.
- ✔ To encourage our pupils to participate in healthy activities.
- ✔ To help our pupils to accept the increasing responsibility they have for maintaining their own health.

Some of these probably dovetail into other content areas of the national PSHE guidance more generally, and may helpfully be integrated into other policy statements.

Programmes of Study

Very little drugs education is compulsory. From September 2000 in England and Wales, the National Curriculum science Order requires the following (Key Stage 3 content is included here to show the progression for which teachers need to prepare Key Stage 2 pupils):

At Key Stage 1

✔ pupils should be taught about the role of drugs as medicines.

At Key Stage 2

✔ pupils should be taught about the effects of tobacco, alcohol and other drugs, and how these relate to their personal health.

At Key Stage 3

✔ pupils should be taught that the abuse of alcohol, solvents and other drugs affects health, how the growth and reproduction of bacteria and viruses can affect health, and how the body's natural defence may be enhanced by immunisation and medicines.

There are other required elements which, while not specifying drugs, have relevance to drug education.

Schools are at liberty to decide how the drug education *requirements* should be taught, (which are not required to be in the context of science), and what *additional content*, in any, will be included. Readers should inspect the new curriculum and frameworks which can be found at: http://www.nc.uk.net

In the new curriculum proposals, slight changes of wording do not alter the content of these requirements. Schools are at liberty to decide how this minimum requirement should be taught, which need not be in the context of Science, and whether anything additional will be included.

In Scotland, references in the 5–14 curriculum guidance to 'Health Education: Healthy and Safe Living' include: 'Activities should encourage pupils to develop a sense of responsibility for their own health ...'. Key features of **Looking after oneself** for Stages P4 to P7 refer to 'the relative risk to health of specific activities and situations such as smoking, drinking alcohol, solvent abuse, drug use, and how to minimise levels of risk in risky situations.' The **Relationships** section refers to '... people and agencies who can provide help ...' at Stages P4 to P6, and 'the powerful influence of peer and media pressure and the relationship between independence and responsibility' at Stage P7. **Health and Safety in the Environment** specifies cigarette smoke as a potential environmental risk, and tobacco advertising as an issue having a bearing on health. **Attainment Targets** specify, at Level B, the importance of finding out about the views of peers and familiar adults on specific health issues, and, at Level E, of exploring stereotypes, including 'drug pusher' and 'alcoholic'.

SCAA guide

Here is a summary of non-statutory content from the SCAA guide on drugs education (listed as item 5 on p.27).

Knowledge and understanding

At Key Stage 1 (age 5–7), the emphasis is on understanding the body, the sources and uses of medicines, safety rules and people who can provide help when needed. At Key Stage 2 (age 8–11), suggestions include some consideration of other drugs, both legal and illegal, the laws governing them, and the dangers of handling syringes.

Skills

At Key Stage 1, it is important for children to be able to communicate concerns, follow instructions and seek help. At Key Stage 2, their needs widen to encompass more general communication skills with peers and adults, identifying risks, giving and getting help, and decision-making and assertiveness in situations involving drugs.

Attitudes

Key Stage 1 pupils should be encouraged to value their bodies and consider how they think of medicines and medical professionals, the use of alcohol and tobacco and how they respond to media treatment of these drugs. At Key Stage 2, pupils have a growing need to take responsibility for themselves, to value self and others and to explore attitudes and beliefs about drugs and drug users.

Many further suggestions are to be found in primary school drugs education resources.

PSHE – the natural home

Teachers are sometimes fearful that their pupils are too young for some of the recommended content of drugs education but they should have confidence in their own judgement about what is appropriate. Starting where pupils are is another safety device – check beforehand that your work relates to the current level of pupils' understanding, or use pupils' responses to determine direction and depth of a lesson as it progresses.

The non-statutory framework for personal, social and health education and citizenship at Key Stages 1 and 2 provide relevant guidance here. In the section on *Developing a healthy, safer lifestyle*, at Key Stage 1, the framework states that pupils should be taught:

- that all household products, including medicines, can be harmful if not used properly

and at Key Stage 2, it states that pupils should be taught:

- what makes a healthy lifestyle, including the benefits of exercise and healthy eating, what affects mental health, and how to make informed choices
- which commonly available substances and drugs are legal and illegal, their effects and risks

- that pressure to behave in an unacceptable or risky way can come from a variety of sources, including people they know, and how to ask for help and use basic techniques for resisting pressure to do wrong
- school rules about health and safety, basic emergency aid procedures and where to get help.

Discussion topics

Circumstances where medicines are encountered may already be familiar to pupils: to raise issues of *safety* in this context may seem more natural and helpful to pupils than if particular attention is focused upon the idea of *danger*, with no apparent reason other than teacher fear.

Exploring the ways in which peer influence works, which may as often be in desirable ways as not, can be done in a manner which considers a range of features such as fashion, respect, negotiation, rules, expectations, adventure, impression, personal resolve, without putting the spotlight upon any particular one without good reason.

Real-life incidents

Often a good strategy for raising issues sensitively and appropriately is to respond to an incident, idea or news item brought by one of the pupils, by eliciting further ideas, questions, concerns, or viewpoints from the children themselves. In this way, specific issues can be dealt with against a general background whose relevance has been set by the pupils.

There may be little need for trepidation about planning 'The Drugs Education Lesson'. Personal, Social and Health Education can act as the catch-all arena for this or any of the other issues which, through exploring and building upon current awareness, and increasing skills and confidence, help pupils to deal with a range of real-life situations they may face now or later.

Training

Established skills

As much concern has been expressed by primary teachers about their lack of expertise on the subject of drugs as upon their quite appropriate reticence to address the subject too early. The issue of training and support is an important one for colleagues whose initial teacher training probably did not set out to equip them in this respect.

However, many of the established skills primary teachers have which deal competently with the normal growth and development of the under 11s are as relevant to drugs education as anything that further training can provide. Confidence in practised skills, such as those mentioned on p.30, is therefore entirely appropriate. Some relevant teaching methods are outlined later in this chapter.

Methodology

Rationale

It is by actively involving young people in their PSHE that they will be likely to learn most. In recent times, there has been renewed concentration on precisely defined programmes of study throughout the school curriculum, placing the emphasis upon content rather than process, perhaps tending to concentrate on children as recipients rather than participants.

In PSHE, there are two vital factors which free teachers from such a strait-jacket.

Firstly, there is no statutory content prescribed for PSHE, though non-statutory guidelines on content are given in the new PSHE framework.

Secondly, the significance of skills acquisition and practice, and the need to explore and consider attitudes and values as they affect decisions, behaviours and responses, mean that pupils cannot be mere recipients of information. They need to develop a sound understanding of themselves and their lives, and to become competently responsible for their behaviour and their welfare. Their participation in their learning is perhaps more important in PSHE than anywhere else in the school curriculum. It is therefore helpful to focus principally upon the *process* of PSHE rather than consider it as a mere syllabus. Research has shown that children prefer project work and class debates, and are much less keen on worksheets, writing tasks, or long periods of reading or listening.

Much of the rest of this chapter will therefore comment upon a variety of classroom methods which can involve pupils interactively, providing opportunities for them to consider their feelings and their own viewpoints in the light of their experience, as they learn about life and about the drugs that they might meet along its path.

Processing

This attempt to help pupils to identify and explore the significance of what they have been doing in a lesson is often called processing. It will frequently be during this follow-up discussion, *which should be a part of every PSHE lesson*, that the most significant learning will take place.

Open-ended questions

The best prompts are often open-ended questions, recognising individual views rather than seeking one 'right' answer. Relevance and learning will frequently differ from pupil to pupil and this is not only appropriate, it is quite inevitable. A skilled teacher may probe and prompt in order to bring about particular insight, but beware of giving the message that only one view or impression should be taken from any input or experience, still less that this should necessarily accord with your own. To acknowledge any diversity of response and opinion that emerges will have the effect of recognising and respecting individual difference, and will encourage children to think for themselves rather than try to guess what you are thinking or simply to say what they think you want them to say.

Thinking time

'Thinking time' is important, too. An obvious pause after a request for a response has been put will tell pupils that you are genuinely wanting them to think and then answer. 'I can see you're still thinking about this' can punctuate a wait without adding pressure.

Jugs and Herrings

This endearing term is affectionately used to describe the result of a highly significant piece of research conducted in 1986 by the (then) Health Education Council's Primary Schools Project at Southampton University. The research was significant for two reasons. Firstly, it told us more than we had ever known before about what young children knew about drugs in Southampton and Nottingham in 1986. Secondly, and more importantly, it can be replicated in any primary school classroom to find out what your own pupils know, now.

The research

The research[4] (see p.63) was carried out with children aged 4–11, asking them to draw (and write if they could) answers to five key questions. They were told a story about Cheryl, who was walking home one day when she found a bag with drugs inside it. These were the five questions, in outline:

- ✔ What do you think was in the bag?
- ✔ Who do you think lost it?
- ✔ What do you think the person was going to do with it?
- ✔ What did Cheryl do with the bag?
- ✔ What would you have done if you had found it?

Their drawings were illuminating indeed, telling us that even some of the very youngest pupils have some idea what the word 'drug' means and that by age eleven they often have a quite intricate understanding of the world of drugs as one including some dangerous and forbidden substances, with sad and needy people among their users. Some of the very young pupils thought 'drugs' was 'jugs' and that they were being asked about a word (perhaps heroin) that they had heard, which sounded a bit like 'herring' which they knew was a fish. These they dutifully drew, inviting the research's nickname!

The findings

From this research, a picture emerged of growing children slowly accumulating awareness of medicines, alcohol, tobacco and the illicit drugs, and their social and legal status, from overheard conversations, television, newspapers, older siblings, their observation and their own experience. This conflicted with the rather more simplistic assumption of children being 'innocent' until the uncomfortable (for teachers) moment arrived when they had to be introduced to knowledge about drugs for their own protection. The emerging view of primary school drugs education as a slow developmental process has been based, to a considerable degree, upon the discoveries of Jugs and Herrings.

Its greatest value today is that to repeat it in your own classroom can tell you with some precision how much your pupils know, where the gaps and misunderstandings lie and what they are now ready to hear and explore. This is a far more important guide to relevant starting points than any printed guidance produced for an entire nation. It is worth seeking out.

TV, video, CD-ROM

It can be tempting to assume that professionally produced resources contain material of a similarly high standard and sitting children down to receive 'expert input' from such media may feel attractive, even an easy option for a busy teacher. In reality, not all high quality productions contain appropriate material and the only way to discover this is to view the material and assess its place, if any, in your work. Pre-record television programmes, and view videos carefully before deciding whether to purchase. Criteria for assessment of any drug-related resource are listed on p.45.

Follow up

One advantage of a recording is that pausing, repeating, omitting and re-ordering are all possible. In any case, the golden rule is always: follow up. Asking pupils to reflect upon what they have seen and to explore its relevance *for them* can aid learning. Suitable open-ended questions may include these:

- ✔ What did you find interesting about the programme/video? Why was that?
- ✔ What purpose do you think the maker had in mind?
- ✔ If you had been (in that scene) what would you have done?
- ✔ What other things could you do or say (in that situation)?
- ✔ What have you learned from the programme/video and what from our discussion?

The use of '... do you think' and '... did you find' seek points of view rather than 'right' answers. Use closed questions only to draw attention to important facts.

CD-ROMs

The same advice to 'know your material' applies to CD-ROMs. They will be far more effective if they are truly interactive, requiring considered responses from a pupil rather than simply a choice of paths through an information presentation. CD-ROMs which can be regulated by the teacher to restrict pupils to selected material can help to direct individual research for a pupil seeking information to bring back to others.

Disadvantages include the fact that monitoring a pupil's progress and learning can be hard, and each machine will serve only one pupil, or a small group, at a time. Always consider carefully the context within which they are used. CD-ROMs are unlikely to be effective unless there is both high motivation and staying power. Novelty value may not last.

All such media are an adjunct to more active classwork with teacher support, not a substitute.

Didactic presentation

Wrongly frowned upon as a somewhat passive learning tool, this has value as a straightforward and often efficient information provider. Where pupils' own processing of ideas is of such great importance, PSHE needs to provide a variety of opportunities which involve, challenge, give space for reflection, allow discussion, take account of experience, court reassessment and change of stance, and mix verbal, non-verbal and written responses to a range of stimuli in individual, small and whole-class settings. Problems can therefore arise if didactic input predominates – principally through loss of interest and therefore impact.

Carefully chosen modes of input, such as teacher talk, pupil presentation of research, television or school nurse talk, can both ring the changes and offer a punchy source of valuable facts. The trick is to make input short and relevant, and time it to follow activity or an expression of raised interest to maximise attention and receptiveness. Always follow up to assess impact and response. Avoid long lists of dos and don'ts, or a complex series of facts which are unlikely to be memorable.

Exploring attitudes and discussing issues

If you invite pupil openness without ground rules, minority views may be belittled and shyness encouraged. Only when there is no fear of ridicule will true openness emerge. Ground rules are therefore required, though it is essential that they are generated by the class members (of whom the teacher is but one) and that the significance of each item is clarified and agreed, with periodic review as necessary. It is also important for there to be shared responsibility for maintaining the standards demanded by the rules and consensus about what will be done if they are breached. Ground rules from a junior class are reproduced on p.8 of *Curriculum Guidance 5: Health Education* (listed as item 3 on p.27).

Range of views

To explore pupils' attitudes, first elicit a range of views. For example, with older pupils, invite the class to brainstorm things that come into their heads when they hear the word 'risk'. Record carefully, noting the difference between *situational* ideas (stealing, shouting at Dad, patting strange dogs) *qualitative* words (naughty, fun) and possible *outcomes* (get into trouble, get hurt, lose face). Attitudes to risk will naturally vary from pupil to pupil according to such factors as inadequate understanding or varying levels of adventurousness. Keep in mind that the concept is not a simple or straightforward one even for adults, who may climb high peaks, exceed speed limits or drink too much, and can be prone to confusing danger with mere disapproval.

Incomplete sentence

A second strategy is to start with an incomplete sentence such as: 'It is risky if you ...' and ask the children to complete it individually or in groups. Slips collected in can ensure anonymity, subsequent discussion permitting conflicting views and probing to find out what is meant or why an individual holds a particular opinion. This can be very powerful in getting children to think for themselves, to challenge each other and to re-assess their standpoints.

Vivid stimulus

At the other end of the age range, try starting with a vivid stimulus, such as a scenario from a story book, and give opportunities to the children to say how they feel about it, and its characters and what they think might–could–should happen next. From this, a discussion can be directed into children's own lives by using words like, 'Supposing ...'.

Example

Gina was talking to her friend Josie as they walked out into the playground at the beginning of playtime.
'I like your bag. I want one like that.'
'Well you can't have mine. My Mum gave it to me.'
'I don't want yours, anyway. My Dad can get me a blue one if I ask him.'
Gina paused and then asked, 'What's in it?'
'My story book and an apple and my purse with 80p inside.'
Gina's eyes opened a bit wider. She knew they weren't supposed to bring money to school.
'Don't tell Miss Weston, or you'll be in trouble! What are you going to spend it on?'
'Sweets. At the sweet shop down the road.'
'Can I come?'
'OK, as long as you don't tell. If we go now when they're not looking, we can be back before playtime's over.'
Gina's eyes opened wider still and her eyebrows almost disappeared under her fringe ...

What will Gina do? What would happen if she ...? The pupils' answers can make Gina strong or weak, daring or cautious, good or naughty, and explore the different scenarios that could ensue. Will Josie be susceptible to reason or is her mind made up? Is she trying to impress Gina? Does she just want a friend? How do people pick friends ...? What else might be in the bag? and so on. You probably need not seek or emphasise a 'right' outcome to the story; instead, try to chair a discussion considering the consequences so that the pupils conclude what happens next. Allowing difference of view, emphasis, or detail is part of supporting individual children to feel that they are trusted to think and act sensibly without always being told what to do, though your judgement will always be there if needed to decide precisely when to 'chair' and when to intervene. The story can be adapted as you go.

Avoid introducing drugs into Josie's bag if very young children omit them. Further up the school, they may tentatively find cigarettes, medicines, cannabis or other risky things in such fictitious bags, like matches, or things which aren't theirs. Help them to explore these ideas.

Using visitors to help you

Though visitors or outside agencies can have value, great care is needed to integrate their contribution fully into your programme, preferably through team teaching. Visitors are still being asked to deliver drugs education in schools where teachers believe that an 'expert' is required who has greater credibility and confidence than they, often principally to give information about dangers. The value of pure information giving is limited and as soon as exploration and discussion are added, the teacher is usually a better expert.

However, if outside support is used, it should be to add colour, experience or perspective that is valuable and cannot be provided by you. You must then lay down guidelines and boundaries within which the visitor works. Schools remain responsible for everything that is taught. Further guidance is provided on p.6 of DfEE Circular 4/95 and in Annex 4 on p.24 of the same circular (see p.64).

Secondary links

For upper juniors, it may be worth exploring with local secondary school colleagues whether there are any pupils that they could recommend to help to support the transition to the 'big' school. Peer-led drugs education involving training senior pupils to tutor younger pupils is occurring more widely, and effort may be amply repaid if a pair of open, sensitive seniors can be located and enlisted from such a source. Many issues, fears and myths about secondary school life might be addressed this way, which could, as part of the package, consider any of the questions upper junior pupils have about drugs and related local circumstances. Your later follow-up could then help to consolidate this valuable experience. It is worth enquiring whether your local senior school might help in this way.

Work in groups

When children are old enough to be given a task to complete by themselves in a small group, there can be tangible advantages. Speaking in a small group (as long as the groups are ordered in such a way that everyone feels comfortable) may not be so daunting as speaking in front of the whole class. Ground can be covered quite fast when many young brains can pool ideas and several discussions can occur at once, often with enthusiastic feedback to the whole class to follow it.

Group organisation

Well-established ground rules can assist smooth working among any combination of pupils, but beware of putting all 'talkers' together. The class's usual seating arrangement may be a good basis for structured group tasks but varying the combinations can ensure social contact spreads more widely than friendship groups. The level of co-operation with a general instruction like 'Get into groups of three or four' will be some guide as to how ready pupils are for self-selection; beware of hurtful exclusions. Reusable personalised cards displaying several group names or symbols in varying combinations can ensure a series of judiciously engineered groupings.

Individual work

A short period of individual work can ensure that everyone has a contribution to make. An instruction such as 'Draw (or write) three things that you think your parents wouldn't want you to do' could lead to group discussion about disapproval, fairness, health, safety, freedom, limits and rules. A broadly similar range of issues can be raised and discussed at age five as at age eleven, though complexity and perspective will alter as the children grow and as issues are revisited. If drugs figure in their suggestions, be ready for them, but if not, the other issues are all relevant. There is no need to force the pace.

More formal methods

Overall, there is less of a role for more formal methods, such as individual reading and writing exercises, in primary school drugs education, although they have their place, particularly as pupils become more competent in these skills. For example, individual research and feedback can confer status and avoid the teacher always appearing to be the information giver. Individual reflection can also be important but interaction is often the catalyst for personal change. Experience is often its substance.

Puzzles

Avoid puzzles involving finding hidden messages or vaguely relevant words, or colouring pictures of safe or dangerous activities. They may, on occasion, keep children quiet, but probably add little to constructive learning yet, strangely, they are still to be found in otherwise high quality resources. Watch for carelessly judgemental language, which can even work against the feeling of competent responsibility you are trying to foster. Be sensitive to how such activities may link with your aims.

Quizzes

Quizzes which are set by pupil to challenge pupil and plumb knowledge can be fun. However, they are better as a way of consolidating learning rather than introducing it. Material can be restricted to a source of known quality and relevance or be drawn from information that has emerged in previous sessions. One advantage of such quizzes is that they can indicate where learning has occurred and where gaps exist. Another is that language is appropriately crafted by the pupils themselves. A careful look at the 'Knowledge and Understanding' section on p.8 of SCAA's guidance will suggest content that may lend itself to this approach. If questions are to be less restricted, answers will occasionally need vetting, so be prepared to intervene to avoid anything being said which you feel is inappropriate.

A disadvantage can be the simple 'right-or-wrong' nature of facts, though a processing session may add more individual value (or maybe just pronounce the game fun!). Remember that application of knowledge is the significant factor. This is where discussion, allowing consideration of the pupils' own experiences, fears and expectations, is vital. This may be approached through literature or drama.

Literature

The enormous power of children's literature can be harnessed to good effect to deal with a multiplicity of issues in PSHE. It can engage children's imagination and help them to explore their feelings and understanding through the experiences and emotions of characters brought to life through stories. The key is to choose stories which paint realistic and plausible pictures, with the possibilities of open endings and interpretations, rather than those which consist of fairly obvious adult messages masquerading as fiction, which can stifle creativity and individual involvement with the situations they portray. Particularly try to avoid doom and gloom stories telling of the dire consequences of drug-taking, or dealing simplistically with the 'yes or no' choice in responding to peer pressure to take drugs (see Myth 10, p.14).

Story and follow-up

Know your story thoroughly and, if not reading it all, choose a section to read out which sets a vivid scene. Prompt by asking the children what they have understood to be going on, and to say something about each of the characters. You might invite them to draw or write a 'picture' of each, and consider what feelings might be involved in the storyline, what options it presents, what outcomes might occur. Try to draw out their current level of understanding, and add to it from your own wisdom and by carefully chosen prompts which encourage contributions from the class. Some excellent literature has been written to deal with all manner of issues, such as bullying, fear of monsters, the need to be heard, child protection and risk-taking. Their relevance to drugs education should not be underestimated in the hands of the creative teacher. Knowledgeable librarians may help to reduce your browsing time, and the local book shop may yield nuggets of gold to the careful searcher. Drama can further enrich the learning possibilities.

Drama

Drama (or 'Let's pretend!') can be used *ad hoc* to extend the exploration process, and is perhaps potentially the most powerful of all PSHE methods. It has nothing to do with the 'performance' or 'learning lines' of the Christmas play. 'OK Narinda, pretend you're Lisa in the story. What can you make her say to Toni that you think would help? Who'd like to be Toni? OK, Sara. Be ready to answer Lisa; just say what you think Toni would have said. Narinda, how do you think Lisa would be feeling ...?' and so on. Children respond more easily to a fictitious scenario with pretend characters than one which somehow might implicate them. Familiarity with drama techniques breeds ready co-operation. The question: 'How would *you* feel if ...' may be answered by someone filling that person's 'shoes' and for the class to explore how it feels from close up. Temporarily 'freezing' a scene can make a space for discussion, a chosen situation being explored as presented or re-run from a variety of perspectives. Say 'Let's look at that again. But this time ...' with pupils suggesting the changes. Scenes that refuse to resolve in a single, satisfactory way will help to prepare children for real life!

Seize opportunities

The story does not need to come from a book, nor involve great length. If it is simply to stimulate study, it can be made up by you beforehand or even in response to a dilemma that arises during some class discussion. Sometimes potential situations arise unexpectedly and the children can be invited to name the characters and create the background. Alternatively, ask the class to write (verbally for young ones; perhaps in small groups at any age) a story or scene to illustrate a point, and choose from the range of responses.

Avoid confusion

It is important to keep in mind that if one child takes on a role, you ensure the others in the class do not confuse character and player, but instead recognise that the player is exploring the feelings and opinions of someone else. This will be more straightforward if the role is somewhat caricatured (a finger-wagging parent saying 'Stop that at once!') but harder for some class members if, say, a male classmate 'plays' a fictitious boy his own age with quite different opinions.

It is also essential to 'de-role' the players after using these techniques by, for instance, inviting them to tell the class their name and something else which makes them different from the character they were playing, and then to ensure there are no emotional leftovers from the scene just played.

Materials for drugs education

There are now many good quality teaching resources for primary schools to be found which wholly or partly deal with drugs. The Jugs and Herrings exercise can help you to decide if children are ready for explicit work on drugs, and where the gaps, questions, inaccuracies, stereotypes and fears are to be found, which will go a long way to determine starting points. It is worth mentioning again that, although drugs-specific work can be appropriate and needed, there is often much to be said for the subject not to be dealt with in isolation from other health, risk, and legitimacy issues. This ensures that a developmental basis relating to young lives can be seen as the motivation, rather than what might be construed as simple adult preoccupation, which may reduce interest and even credibility, particularly amongst older pupils.

It is therefore useful to look at more general PSHE resources for material dealing generally with health, responsibility, help, and skills needed to cope with a range of situations, alongside their treatment of drugs. These can be augmented from material in drugs-specific packs. Some examples are listed on p.63.

Assessing materials

Careful assessment is important. *The Right Choice* (see item 10 on p.28), published jointly in 1998 by the Standing Conference on Drug Abuse and the Drug Education Forum, lists key criteria for good drugs education materials, developed from research, evaluation and expert opinion.

Key criteria

- ✔ Clearly stating underpinning beliefs and values.
- ✔ Showing how the materials incorporate pupils' existing drug awareness.
- ✔ Offering a range of activities, based on successful teaching and learning styles.
- ✔ Giving accurate and balanced facts, not aiming to shock or horrify.
- ✔ Assessing aims and objectives.
- ✔ Including examples of how the materials meet statutory and non-statutory learning outcomes.
- ✔ Cross-referencing to target ages, National Curriculum key stages and cross-curricular subjects.
- ✔ Guiding on the knowledge, understanding and skills needed to deliver the material.
- ✔ Recognising the importance of parental understanding, support and involvement.
- ✔ Providing evidence of successful use in schools.

This very useful booklet expands upon each criterion in turn and provides a fuller checklist to assist assessment of the relevance and quality of materials.

Chapter

5

A partnership with parents

The involvement of parents

It is important for parents to know the approach their children's school is taking to address the subject of drugs, and for them to feel confidence in it. Their level of knowledge about drugs is not likely to be detailed unless they have taken the trouble to seek it. Their principal information providers are probably the mass media, which deal too frequently in sensational stories and scaremongering to be of much practical value. The more high-profile political responses generally fuel concern by seeking more effective measures to curb supply, while calmer educational initiatives, despite growing political support, get less media coverage and often escape public attention.

Consequently, mention of the word 'drugs' will tend to bring to parents' minds stories of illegal dealing and extreme problems, such as long-term addiction, which sell newspapers but do little to address their needs in bringing up children.

Hold an open evening

A good starting point for schools wishing to work closely with parents is therefore to organise an evening to address anxieties and to discuss the school's strategy.

If you feel sufficiently resourceful to run such a meeting using only your own staff, it can inspire confidence in parents that you know your subject. However, if you feel support from an outside person may lend status or expertise to the event and even attract a bigger audience, choose someone whose understanding of drugs is matched by their familiarity with the educational issues. If your LEA has a Health Education Co-ordinator or other adviser/advisory teacher with a Health Education brief, this may be the person to ask. If his or her portfolio does not include drugs, a Health Promotion Specialist from the Health Authority may be available. Aim for an educationalist who can give a calm overall perspective on the subject of drugs in order to place the school's initiatives in context.

It will help to have chosen an unsensational title for the meeting, such as 'Drugs and young people: the school and parents working together', which is clear and sounds positive. Even so, expect your audience to include some who consider drugs a plague and want you to help to banish it, and some who are frightened that you will introduce the subject to children too early.

Encourage discussion

Anxiety is likely to be high, so start by allowing parents to say why they have come and what their worries are. Some schools arrange the room with small tables each seating four or five parents, encouraging an informal atmosphere, and making brief group discussions easy to conduct. In this way, more parents may feel they can contribute. If possible, record their comments on a board or flip chart so that each is given recognition. It is important to acknowledge anxieties, not necessarily trying to dispel them, even if some seem to you unrealistically gloomy. However, a balanced picture of the drug 'scene' may provide a more comforting picture than previously held, which may help to prepare the ground for understanding and accepting a developmental approach to the subject with pupils. The main presentation may bring questions to punctuate the talk as well as to follow it and these deserve full attention.

Display resources

It can then be constructive to ask parents, again in groups initially, to consider what the school could do, as a platform for discussing the role of the curriculum. Put on show the resources you use with pupils, and have a copy of the SCAA guidance document to hand, which can help to demonstrate your accordance with the national pattern. Try to ensure that parents take away realistic expectations of you, and that they know that the door is open to discuss the issue with you at any time.

If you decide to produce a separate drugs policy for the school, the evening can constitute early involvement of parents in the development process. Eventual distribution of the policy can help to cement the partnership approach.

Chapter 6

Drugs on school premises

Safety

It is highly recommended that schools put safety at the top of the agenda, which demonstrates to staff, governors, parents and pupils alike the concern for pupil well-being above all else.

One way to do this is to extend management procedures designed to deal with medicines and legal drugs to encompass any circumstance where pupils bring drugs, whether legitimately or otherwise, on to school premises. Medicines, glue and tobacco may be brought on to school premises by staff quite legitimately, as may alcohol on occasion. You may find it helpful to refer to health and safety guidance documents where reference to legal drugs is commonly to be found. Sniffable substances need to be restricted entirely or very carefully controlled along with alcohol, tobacco and supervision of medicines, which pose the commonest serious threat to young people's safety. Medicines may sometimes be brought by pupils.

The legal status of any drug, though significant, need only be ascertained after safety issues have been considered and acted upon. For effective management, the school needs to know about all drugs, whatever their purpose or legal status and whoever has them. They can then be stored, administered, consumed, confiscated, locked away, or destroyed, whichever is appropriate.

Opportunities to educate

Don't forget that every time the presence or use of any drug comes to the attention of a pupil or pupils, it presents an opportunity to discuss it as a part of drugs education. Asthma inhalers or other medicines, the teacher or school visitor who smokes, glue bags found in the street, as well as any pupil misdemeanour all present a chance to discuss, even if only briefly, the use, the social, medical and legal status of the drug, and any attendant rules, laws and safety issues.

Medicines

Medicines brought to school by pupils, whether legitimately or otherwise, generally provide excellent opportunities for drugs education. Medical issues are dealt with in *Managing Medicines in Schools* by Joe Harvey (Folens) and your local General Practitioner/School Paediatric Service can also advise. The National Asthma Campaign also publishes helpful guidance about managing asthma medication during the school day and the DfEE Good Practice Guide *Supporting Pupils with Medical Needs* gives additional guidance including administrative procedures and a series of forms for recording.

Illegal drugs

The cases where an illegal drug is brought on to primary school premises are still relatively uncommon. If illegal drugs are found or suspected at school, or if a pupil is possibly under the influence of any unknown drug, the following procedure is suggested:

Suggested procedure

- ✔ If there seems to be any medical attention needed, seek or provide it at once.
- ✔ Confiscate any drug and ask what it is, in case the pupil loses consciousness and doctors need to know. Give sample to ambulance crew/hospital if required.
- ✔ Ensure that there is a witness to confiscation; store substance; record carefully.
- ✔ Inform Head Teacher/Drugs Issues Co-ordinator.
- ✔ Try to determine the level of seriousness of the incident. This may take time, and will not be as urgent as meeting medical need. There is a huge difference between an accident, a mistake and a wilful transgression, and between possession, taking a drug and involving other pupils.
- ✔ Assess the pupil's (non-medical) need for education, support, sanctions.
- ✔ Consider the needs of any other pupil(s) involved or implicated.
- ✔ Consider informing, consulting or involving outside agencies, e.g. parents, police, LEA. (If possible, choose specialist education officers within police, and Health Education Co-ordinator or equivalent in LEA.)
- ✔ Identify/curtail the source of the drug if you can. Police may have a role at this point, as may Social Services if home is a suspected source.

Remember that, although involving parents is usually a high priority, the law does not demand it, or the involvement of police. Assess carefully, with expert help if needed, what you want to achieve and the best way of bringing it about. You may not search a pupil. Nor is it appropriate to try to identify a drug conclusively. If expertise is needed, do not hesitate to seek it. Your school's drugs policy should specify procedures clearly but leave room for careful judgement relating to individual circumstances. The school is *in loco parentis,* and so has to be seen to act in respect of an individual child as a reasonable, caring parent would act.

Confiscation

Any drug may be confiscated for safety's sake and, more specifically, it is permissible for teachers to confiscate an illegal drug in order to prevent a crime being committed. This should be done with an adult witness, a careful record should be kept, and secure storage arranged if the drug is not to be destroyed immediately (usually by flushing down the toilet). In any case, it is advisable to destroy it or pass it to the police or a doctor within 24 hours.

Support

Explain carefully why any action is being taken. It is important for a pupil to know that your principal concerns are health and safety. Show you care. Though boundaries need to be clear and enforced, too strong an emphasis on rules could be construed as a challenge.

Exclusions

In the rare case of a serious drug-related misdemeanour, fixed-term exclusion is one among many options, though it should always be considered only 'when it is clear that a pupil is selling drugs and the health and safety of other pupils is directly at risk.' Exclusion should only be made permanent as 'a final sanction, when all other reasonable steps have been taken.' The quotes are from DfEE Circular 4/95 (see p.64).

Detailed guidelines for dealing with incidents involving illegal drugs are to be found in DfEE Circular 4/95 and SCODA's guidance booklet, *The Right Responses* (see p.64). Each LEA will also have its own procedures for supporting schools in this sort of predicament. A policy on drugs, which is highly recommended though not compulsory, can be invaluable in providing clarity to staff and parents about how the school intends to respond to incidents of this kind.

In considering how to respond, take care to ensure that the legal status of any drug is not permitted to overtake the highest priorities, which should always be the safety and educational needs of any pupils involved.

Chapter

7

The school drugs policy

The way forward

It is strongly to be encouraged to have your school's stance on the subject of drugs clearly enshrined in print. Some schools include a section in a more general policy such as PSHE, Health and Safety or Pupil Welfare and this may be all that is needed. Though there is no statutory requirement for a drugs policy, the advantages of clarity and consequent consistency are powerful incentives, as is the fact that OFSTED monitors drugs policies as part of their inspection programme. The 1995 Inspection Handbook also says in connection with drugs:

'Inspectors should (also) determine whether schools have clear policies and procedures for ... working with other services concerned with young people to offer appropriate support and advice.'

The range of statutory services, such as Social Services, Police, Health Promotion, Youth and Community, may be mentioned in a section on pupil welfare along with specialists in the voluntary sector, such as counselling services. Though primary schools may seldom have call to consult external services, it is as well to document where support is to be found locally, just in case.

Preparation

Before writing a drugs policy, consider who should be involved in the process. An imposed document which may not reflect their views will be much harder for staff to feel they own. A good strategy can be to call a parents' meeting as described in Chapter 5, put the matter on to the agenda of a governor's meeting, and arrange some in-service training for the staff to help to develop their awareness and skills and boost their confidence, *before* trying to draft the policy. In this way, the policy can build upon any evolution in thinking taking place. A small, volunteer group can then pool all expressed ideas and produce an embryonic draft, to be considered and amended by larger groups as necessary. Others, such as health promotion staff or the school nurse, might also be consulted at some stage.

What to include

A drugs policy should be short, clear, consistent and agreed between everyone involved, addressing:

- ✔ the school's position on drugs
- ✔ general arrangements for the provision of a sensitive, developmental drugs education
- ✔ managing drugs including medicines brought on to school premises
- ✔ pupils' welfare and needs
- ✔ in-service training
- ✔ parents
- ✔ governors.

Involving pupils

You might consider consulting pupils, too, as long as you feel they are ready to contribute. In this case, tell them that a plan is being produced which will help the school to provide the maximum benefit to pupils in respect of the 'world of drugs'. Then ask them to say what they would like teachers to help them learn about drugs, and perhaps what rules the school should have for pupils, and for teachers, about drugs. An exercise of this kind will not tie your hands and it can be illuminating in telling you about pupils' perceptions of the benefit they could derive, may suggest adjustments of content or thrust, and will certainly tell *them* clearly that you are approaching this subject from the perspective of being sensitive to their views.

Appointing a co-ordinator

The policy does not need to cover every eventuality in fine detail; rather it should rely explicitly upon the professional judgement of the staff, and should identify the person who is to take the co-ordinating lead on drugs issues. In small schools, this may well be the Head Teacher, on whose desk the buck eventually stops in any case. The advantages of a co-ordinator include:

- ✔ a reliable reference point for the staff team for curriculum and incident matters
- ✔ a co-ordinated response to training needs
- ✔ a central review of resources, needs and purchases
- ✔ a repository for mail, new publications, circulars for schools
- ✔ a central reference point for new intelligence about drugs, the local 'scene', help sources.

Evaluation

A vital question to ask when it is finished is 'Does it stop us from doing anything we wish to do?' If the answer is no, it is not too restricting. If it inspires confidence and provides the support and clarity on paper which teachers feel they need to do the job, then it is sufficiently enabling. A document will be effective if it is referred to freely and reviewed continually at best and periodically in any case. There is no point in producing a policy which gathers dust on a shelf as it becomes progressively more out of date.

A sample format for the policy

The following example contains suggested headings and content only, as stimulus to individual schools' discussions. It is not intended to replicate a complete policy model.

Drug policy for __________ school

The school's position on drugs

e.g. In this document, the word 'drug' is used to include all drugs whatever their legal or social status, including alcohol, tobacco, solvents and medicines. We recognise that any drug can be potentially hazardous. We strive to increase competence in our pupils in any drug-related situation they may meet, by ... (specify policy, strategy).

Drugs Issues Co-ordinator

The Drugs Issues Co-ordinator for __________ School is __________ .

Drugs education

e.g. Every attempt will be made to ensure that drugs education will be appropriate to the age and needs of pupils. Content and delivery using active methods will follow guidance in DfEE and LEA documents (specify outline content, guidance). The aims of our drugs education are:

(Specify the aims)

Arrangements for the provision of drugs education

e.g. Drugs education will be integrated into Personal, Social and Health Education and will include the requirements of the National Science Curriculum. Teaching resources we use include:

(Specify resources)

continued

Drug policy for ____________ school continued

Drugs on school premises

e.g. Teachers should know of all drugs that come on to school premises for any reason. If medical aid is needed (or might be needed) for any pupil, it will be provided or sought at once. (Co-ordinator) will co-ordinate management of all incidents involving medical and other drugs to minimise hazard and protect health.

(Specify clear and agreed procedures for your school)

Pupils' welfare and needs

e.g. We address carefully the personal and pastoral needs of the pupils in our care. We recognise that asking for help can be hard and that pupils may sometimes have need for sensitive support. The following local services are also available for the school to refer to:

(Specify local agencies and contacts)

Staff training

e.g. We aim to meet the in-service training needs of our staff. (Co-ordinator) will co-ordinate provision of in-service training.

Parents

e.g. We strive to ensure that parents are kept fully informed about the development of our drugs education programme and that their wishes are taken into account in our planning.

(Specify particular arrangements)

Governors

e.g. The governing body of the school has been involved in the development of and supports our drugs policy and is actively involved in our responses to this issue.

(Specify particular arrangements)

More detailed guidance about setting drugs policy is to be found in the guidance document *The Right Responses* (see p.28).

APPENDIX A: A DRUGS GUIDE

This guide gives fuller details of **alcohol, amphetamines, cannabis, paracetamol, solvents and tobacco,** and also includes **anabolic steroids, ecstasy, LSD, 'magic' mushrooms and tranquillisers.** The guide does not include barbiturates, cocaine, GHB, heroin, ketamine or khat, detailed knowledge of which is not commonly relevant at primary school level. Classes refer to the Misuse of Drugs Act 1971. The rough-and-ready price guide (£ = cheapest, ££££ = most expensive) is comparative within the table, so, for example, heroin would rate more than ££££ and caffeine less than £. Prices vary considerably from place to place and over time. Some may be obtained at no cost.

Drug name	**Amphetamine** and amphetamine-like analogues
Price	**£££**
Description	Synthetic stimulants used to treat hyper-activity and chronic tendency to fall asleep. Milder varieties used to treat obesity. 'Street' amphetamine sulphate (powder, pills) invariably illicit.
Legal status	All amphetamines are prescription-only medicines. Most are also Class B. Prepared for injection, they are Class A. A few milder variants are Class C.
Effects short term	A similar effect to that of adrenaline on someone feeling stress in an emergency. Users feel more energetic and confident. Higher doses make users feel 'capable of anything' and stimulate creativity. Anxiety, irritability and restlessness may follow as the body's energy is used up. Effects last 3–4 hours. After they wear off, users feel tired and hungry. Full recovery can take 1–2 days. Frequent high doses can produce delirium, panic and a form of temporary paranoia known as amphetamine psychosis. Severely interrupted sleep and eating patterns may indicate use.
Effects long term	Tolerance develops, tempting users to increase the dose. This in turn makes delusions and paranoid feelings more likely. Prolonged, heavy use exaggerates symptoms. Resultant lack of sleep and nourishment can be serious and raised blood pressure may damage heart and circulation.
Principal dangers/ other implications	Taking too little account of the body's need to replenish sleep and nourishment. Injection of any substance is hazardous unless carefully and hygienically conducted.

Drug name	**Paracetamol**
Price	**£** Sold in packs of 32 (the maximum allowed in a pack since September 1998)
Description	Self-administered painkiller. Pills and cold remedies containing paracetamol commonly sold at medical outlets (Hedex, Lem-Sip, Calpol, Sin-u-tabs, etc.)
Legal status	Legal. Medicines which may be prescribed, or purchased from pharmacies without prescription. Pharmacists try to ensure only appropriate sales.
Effects short term	Dulls pain effectively for up to 4 hours. Repeat doses should not exceed frequency indicated in instructions. When combined with other preparations such as Lem-Sip, the dose may be unwittingly increased to dangerous levels. As few as 15 tablets may be an overdose for an adult. Smaller doses may be lethal for children. Fatal overdoses are recorded each year, many accidental. Irreversible liver damage may occur before medical assistance can help.
Effects long term	No long-term problems with careful, recommended use.
Principal dangers/ other implications	Accidental overdose. Storage within reach of small children who do not understand the function or potential hazards of the drug.

Drug name	**Cannabis**, hashish, marijuana, leaves or derivatives from the Cannabis Sativa plant
Price	**£££**
Description	Leaf or derived resin or oil is typically mixed with tobacco and smoked. Leaf ('herbal' cannabis or 'grass') may be smoked alone. Resin may be mixed in food and eaten.
Legal status	Class B. Hash oil may be Class A, as are all extracted active ingredients from the plant: 'cannabinoids'. Accounts for 90% of all drug offences.
Effects short term	Effects start a few minutes after smoking and may last an hour or more. Dependent largely on users' moods and expectations, most don't find much to enjoy at first and have to learn to 'steer' the experience. Relaxation and a heightened sense of colour, sound and taste may follow with a state of well-being. Short-term memory loss is commonly reported as are giggling and hunger. Higher doses alter sense of time and other perceptual distortions and can cause confusion and distress.
Effects long term	No conclusive evidence of physical damage. Inhalation of smoke is likely to contribute to respiratory disorders (though quantities used are likely to be significantly smaller than tobacco and the dangers consequently less). Chronic use may lead to apathy and poor general performance and can aggravate existing or latent mental illness.
Principal dangers/ other implications	Use when not feeling 'in harmony' with self or surroundings. Driving while affected. Developing a frequent heavy pattern of use. Getting caught.

Drug name	**Solvents** and other volatile and sniffable substances such as butane gas, glue, toluene, acetone, fluorocarbons (propellants from aerosols), trichloroethane (cleaning fluid), petrol
Price	**££** Varies according to product; often accessible at home
Description	Gases and volatile substances giving off heavy vapour, inhaled from high pressure containers (fire extinguishers, lighter fuel canisters, aerosols) or sniffed from plastic bags (glue, thinners) or soaked material (thinners, poppers) to produce intoxication.
Legal status	The Intoxicating Substances Supply Act 1985 operates in England, Wales and Northern Ireland to restrict retailers from supplying solvents to anyone under 18 if they have reason to believe they will be used for purposes of intoxication. Scotland has broadly similar arrangements under common law. Possession and use of solvents is not an offence, but in some areas bye-laws allow police to take sniffers in public to 'a place of safety'. In Scotland, they can be taken into care. Butane sales to under 18s are illegal in the UK.
Effects short term	Effects similar to alcohol, but shorter lived (typically 10–20 minutes). Vapour absorbed through lungs quickly reaches the brain. Reduced oxygen contributes to the effect. Co-ordination and balance quickly impaired. Reduced inhibition leads to merriment and boisterousness. Deep inhalation can cause unconsciousness, though full recovery is usually quick. Toxic effects of e.g. lighter fuel have killed. Most deaths due to circumstances of sniffing (see 'principal dangers' below).
Effects long term	Long-term, heavy use of 10 years or so may lead to some brain damage. Similar patterns of sniffing aerosols or cleaning fluids have caused kidney and liver damage.
Principal dangers/ other implications	Five distinct hazards leading to fatalities. Sniffing from large plastic bag causing suffocation. Loss of balance from tree, high window, canal bank, etc. Freezing of airways resulting from squirting substance into mouth/nose direct from pressurised container. Exertion after sniffing causing stress to the heart. Vomiting following loss of consciousness.

Drug name	**Alcohol** (principally ethyl alcohol)
Price	**£££** Variable according to strength, source, quantity
Description	Swallowed as a drink. Subject to licensing regulations. Strength varies from product to product, but must be shown on labelling.
Legal status	Possession and use legal at age 5+. Purchase of beer, cider, perry permitted at age 14 in licensed restaurants to drink with a meal. Purchase from licensed premises (pub, off-licence) permitted from age 18. Sale to under 18s forbidden on these premises. Possession an offence on some trains, etc. to designated sporting events.
Effects short term	Absorbed into bloodstream after 5–10 minutes. Effect of one 'unit' (glass of wine, half pint of ordinary beer, single measure of spirits) lasts for approx. 1 hour. Small doses cause light-headedness, relaxation and reduced inhibition. Larger doses progressively impair judgement, balance and co-ordination, cause vomiting, severe reduction of mental and physical function and can lead to unconsciousness. Small people affected more. Death from acute alcohol poisoning possible if dose large enough. Lowered inhibition often contributes to violent or other criminal behaviour.
Effects long term	Obesity and physical damage to brain, liver, kidneys only visible after substantial tolerance and dependence have developed. Also disruption of lifestyle, aggravating personal, social and financial problems. Foetal damage possible for heavy drinking pregnant mothers.
Principal dangers/ other implications	Any situation demanding control and judgement, e.g. driving or balance. Poisoning for small or unhabituated person. Heavy use often accompanied by poor diet. Possibility of addiction.

Drug name	**Tobacco containing nicotine**, Nicorette, Nicotinelle patches
Price	Cigarettes: **££** Patches: **£££**
Description	Products containing dried leaves of tobacco plant. Usually burned and smoke inhaled. Can be chewed or sucked. Cannabis cigarettes ('joints','spliffies') usually contain tobacco as main ingredient. Patches sold to aid withdrawal.
Legal status	Legal to possess and smoke at any age. Supply restricted to licence holders, who may not sell to under 16s, though purchase by under 16s not restricted! Personal cultivation permitted. Use banned in many public places. Park keepers and police officers still permitted to confiscate tobacco from under 16s.
Effects short term	Nicotine is absorbed rapidly by the lungs to reach the brain. Each inhalation has the same rapid, distinct effect, increasing heart rate and blood pressure and stimulating/ arousing the user's nervous system, causing smokers to feel a reduction in stress and anxiety. First use often causes sick and dizzy feelings. Withdrawal causes restless irritability and depression, tempting further use.
Effects long term	Nicotine is addictive. The development of tolerance and dependence are marked and rapid. The more one smokes, the more likely are heart disease, blood clots, bronchitis, lung cancer, cancer of mouth and throat. 111,000 premature deaths occur each year in the UK from smoking-related disorders. If no irreversible damage has occurred, smokers may return to full health and life-expectancy by stopping.
Principal dangers/ other implications	Premature death. Passive smoking now considered a significant risk. Smaller, less mature babies born to smoking mothers. Diseases caused by oral contraceptives ten times more likely among smokers.

Drug name	**Anabolic steroids**
Slang names	Steroids, 'roids
Brand names	Dianabol, Stanozolol, Durabolin, etc.
Group	Stimulants
Price	**££££**
Description	Hormones mostly derived from testosterone, and used to treat anaemia, thrombosis and weakened muscles. Used non-medically to build up muscle bulk.
Legal status	Prescription-only medicines, and Class C. Possession for personal use without prescription is not an offence.
Effects short term	Often used by athletes/bodybuilders in doses far greater than therapeutically recommended. Reports of steroid-induced aggression ('roid rage) are common, opinions differ about whether this is a result of the drugs. Also, no conclusive evidence about whether increased muscle strength derives from steroids or an aggressive outlook by determined improvers.
Effects long term	Side effects are difficult to replicate clinically because athletes' doses are often unethically high. Reports include: liver abnormalities, tumours, hypertension, stunted growth, low sperm counts, temporary psychiatric problems, psychological dependence, (rare) permanent enlargement of male breasts with some steroids, increased female sex drive and enlarged clitoris, permanent female growth of facial and body hair, deepening voice and decrease in breast size – which all may be passed to a foetus by a pregnant user. Sharing needles can pass infections.
Principal dangers/ other implications	Considerable and sometimes permanent physical changes. No improvement in athletic strength or performance. Injection is always hazardous unless careful and hygienic.

Drug name	**LSD** – lysergic acid diethylamide
Slang names	Acid, trips, tabs
Brand names	None
Group	Hallucinogens
Price	**£££**
Description	Powerful drug altering perceptual function. Derived from a fungus, ergot. Taken in tiny tablets or absorbed into small squares of paper or gelatine sheets.
Legal status	Class A under the Misuse of Drugs Act.
Effects short term	Effects (known as a 'trip') begin within 30–60 minutes and typically last around 12 hours. Senses are distorted and perceptions are greatly altered. Trips relate to mood and may be wonderful, uplifting, mystical or strange and terrible. True hallucinations seem rare. Concentration and capability impaired. Trips cannot be stopped once they have started.
Effects long term	No known physical dangers. Adverse psychological reactions have been reported usually in people with some mental instability. Tolerance develops rapidly but not physical dependence. Psychological dependence is rare.
Principal dangers/ other implications	Psychotic episodes for users with latent or embryonic mental illness. Flashbacks (trips relived briefly at later times) can be disorientating. Misjudging time or mood.

Drug name	**Ecstasy**: 3, 4, methylene-dioxymethamphetamine, known as 'MDMA'
Slang names	E, XTC, Dennis the Menace, Love Doves, Disco Biscuits
Brand names	None
Group	Stimulants; technically, ecstasy is a hallucinogenic amphetamine
Price	**£££££**
Description	Usually coloured pills or capsules, illicitly manufactured. Pills may have motif moulded into them, e.g. dove. Capsules may have different coloured ends, e.g. red and black – 'Dennis the Menace'.
Legal status	Class A under the Misuse of Drugs Act. No medical uses.
Effects short term	Strong stimulant. Early effects include tightening of the jaw, brief nausea, sweating and dry mouth, followed by feelings of alertness, euphoria, serenity and calmness, and empathy towards those around. Full effects may take up to an hour to emerge. Around 50 deaths to date have occurred directly associated with ecstasy. Most symptoms seem to have been similar to acute heat-stroke. Some have been heart attack or brain haemorrhage following high blood pressure due to the stimulant effect. Excessive intake of water has been noted in two or three deaths, made worse by ecstasy's capacity to reduce flow of water through the body.
Effects long term	Tolerance develops but not physical dependence. There is some evidence of liver damage among ecstasy users. No evidence of foetal damage, but women with history of genito-urinary tract infection should avoid this drug as should anyone with heart disease, high blood pressure, glaucoma, epilepsy or in poor mental or physical shape.
Principal dangers/ other implications	Overheating and dehydration, due to combined effect of drug and sweating from exertion, e.g. dancing in an enclosed space with others. Effects of long-term use as yet unknown but seems to increase the chance of physiological problems observed so far.

Drug name	**'Magic' (hallucinogenic) mushrooms**
Slang names	'shrooms, mushies
Brand names	None
Group	Hallucinogens
Price	**£** Most commonly gathered from the wild rather than purchased
Description	Liberty Cap and Fly Agaric; indigenously growing mushrooms with hallucinogenic properties. 20–30 Liberty Caps may be needed for an extensive 'trip'.
Legal status	Possession/consumption not restricted. Making 'a preparation or other product' by drying, cooking or infusing them renders them Class A.
Effects short term	Similar to a mild LSD 'trip' often including euphoria and giggling. Shorter (4–9 hours) and quicker to start than LSD. Larger doses may cause stomach pains and vomiting. Anxious or stressed user may be more likely to have a 'bad' trip or even a psychotic episode. Negative effects are temporary.
Effects long term	As with LSD, tolerance develops. Much higher doses may be needed if the experience is to be repeated soon. This diminishes after a week or so. Little evidence of long-term harm, though psychological dependence is a possibility.
Principal dangers/ other implications	Eating deadly poisonous varieties in error. (No deaths yet recorded.)

Drug name	**Tranquillisers** (term usually refers to minor tranquillisers, the benzodiazepines), includes temazepam and diazepam
Slang names	Tranx, moggies, mazzies
Brand names	Valium, Ativan, Mogadon, etc.
Group	Depressants
Price	**££** Purchased usually by prescription, with standard charges
Description	The most commonly prescribed drugs in Britain, used to treat insomnia, anxiety, and mental distress.
Legal status	Prescription-only medicines and in Class C. Possession of any tranquilliser except temazepam without prescription is not itself an offence unless the drug has been illicitly produced.
Effects short term	Depress mental activity, cause drowsiness and forgetfulness, and impair driving skills, though only until habituation (a week or two of continuous use). Relief of anxiety and tension is pleasurable, but not for non-anxious users, hence the relative lack of popularity among young people seeking excitement. High doses bring sleep, which can last into the following day. Overdose is rare, due to number needed (far more than with barbiturates). However, mixing with alcohol lowers the fatal dose.
Effects long term	Tolerance and dependence, probably principally psychological in nature, develop within weeks. Medical effectiveness significantly reduced, or absent, within months. Withdrawal can cause great anxiety even when medical benefit is no longer gained from use. Withdrawal symptoms include insomnia, anxiety, irritability and vomiting. Approx. 13,400,000 prescriptions in 1997 in England alone (*Prescription Cost Analysis – England 1997,* Dept. of Health). Estimates suggest 1,000,000 addicts among these.
Principal dangers/ other implications	Mixing with alcohol; long-term dependence. Leaving within reach of small children. Observed regular intake may set example to young people.

APPENDIX B: FURTHER ADVICE

The general role of primary schools

Most key information is to be found in the documents listed on pp.26–29. If you need clarification of further advice, contact your LEA or Scottish Local Authority first. The person with the health and drugs education portfolio may well be a Health Education Co-ordinator or Advisory Teacher with specialist experience. There may be local guidance about education, management of incidents or formulation of policy. If so, make sure that staff know how such guidance can be accessed, and that, if it is printed, there is a copy in school. Resources aimed at primary schools often have a general section in their early pages addressing the needs of primary school teachers and the contribution their schools can make.

Information about drugs

Drugs information is continually updated by research and in the light of experience. Reliable and objective data, gathered world-wide, can be obtained from the Institute for the Study of Drug Dependence (ISDD) in London. ISDD publishes regularly revised editions of *Drug Abuse Briefing* which provides a comprehensive summary of what is known to date and is strongly recommended as a reference document for teachers. ISDD, Waterbridge House, 32–36 Loman Street, London SE1 0EE. Telephone: 020 7928 1211.

Information about drug laws

Contact RELEASE, an organisation specialising in publications and support on legal matters relating to drugs. RELEASE, 388 Old Street, London EC1V 9LT. Telephone: 020 7729 9904.

Information about developments in drugs education in England and Wales

The Drug Education Forum was formed in 1994 and brings together a broad range of organisations with a variety of perspectives and develops concerns about drugs education issues. It aims to provide an independent and authoritative voice for drugs education. Contact the Co-ordinator, c/o National Children's Bureau, 8 Wakley Street, London EC1V 7QE. Telephone: 020 7843 6000.

The Drug Education Practitioners' Forum is an independent forum for professionals working in drugs education, providing a network for sharing information and experience about drugs education practice and developments in the field. Contact the Chair, Drug Education Practitioners' Forum, c/o SCODA. Telephone: 020 7928 9500.

In-service training

Try first your LEA and the Health Promotion Unit, which is part of the local health authority. In England and Wales, if local expertise is hard to locate, contact the National Health Education Group (NHEG) whose members are principally Health Education Co-ordinators. The NHEG Membership Secretary can put you in touch with your nearest drug issues trainer. National Health Education Group, c/o 103 Northcourt Avenue, Reading, Berks RG2 7HG. Telephone: 0118 975 6528.

Leaflets – *England*

The National Drugs and Solvents Publicity Campaign produces leaflets aimed at 11–14 year olds, which could be used with the top class in primary schools, and leaflets for parents which may be useful at parents' evenings. There is no charge for schools in England. Contact the Drugs-Campaign Ordering Service (D-COS) Telephone: 01304 614731.

Wales

In Wales, leaflets produced for pupils and published by the Welsh Drug and Alcohol Unit are available in bulk from local Health Promotion Units.

Scotland

In Scotland, contact your Health Promotion Department, the Scottish Drugs Forum (see below), or the Health Education Board for Scotland (HEBS). Telephone: 0131 536 5500. HEBS publishes a useful Scottish booklet called *The Facts of Drugs – A Parents' Guide.*

Solvents and sniffing

The Volatile Substance Misuse Project has specialists dealing with all aspects of volatile substance sniffing and education on the subject. Contact the project, c/o National Children's Bureau, 8 Wakley Street, Islington, London EC1V 7QE. Telephone: 020 7843 6000.

Confidential help face-to-face

For the whereabouts of more generic local counselling services aimed at supporting young people in all parts of the UK, contact Youth Access, 1A Taylors Yard, 67 Alderbrook Road, London SW12 8AD.
Telephone: 020 8772 9900. Youthlink Scotland supports member organisations. Telephone: 0131 229 0339.

Drug Action Teams

Every small region has a Drug Action Team and additionally, in England and Wales, one or more Drug Reference Groups covering smaller areas within it. These multi-agency groups consider and co-ordinate local action to combat drug problems and may be able to offer limited financial support.

Help in relation to drugs

England: The National Drugs Helpline is a confidential telephone helpline open 24 hours a day. Telephone: 0800 776600.
Details of local specialist drug support services can be obtained from the Standing Conference on Drug Abuse (SCODA), 32–36 Loman Street, London SE1 0EE. Telephone: 020 7928 9500.

Wales: The Welsh Drug and Alcohol Unit, 4th Floor, St. David's House, Wood Street, Cardiff CF1 1EY provides details of drugs services in Wales. Telephone: 01222 667766.

Scotland: The Scottish Drugs Forum, 5 Waterloo Street, Glasgow G2 6AY provides details of drugs services in Scotland. Telephone: 0141 221 1175.

APPENDIX C: REFERENCES

[1] Parker, Measham, Aldridge; 1996 figures from their study of young people in north-west England. Earlier data published as *Drug Futures*, ISDD, 1995.

[2] Report on the myth of drug-laced tattoos 'LSD: the memory lingers on', *Druglink* magazine, ISDD, Nov/Dec 1995.

[3] Coggans and McKellar, *Health Promoting Schools*, Hobsons Publishing, 1996. See Chapter 2, p.9 'What is Peer Pressure?'

[4] The method for conducting the research eliciting children's perceptions of 'The World of Drugs' is described in detail as 'The Draw and Write investigation technique' in Appendix 1 of Williams, Wetton and Moon, *Health for Life: 2*, Nelson, 1989.

Primary drugs education resources

Brown and Bennett, *The Good Health Guide to Drugs: Resource Book*, Channel 4 Schools, 1996.
Short drugs education guide with activities for 9–12 year-olds, originally published to accompany the Channel 4 Schools programmes.

Cohen, *The Primary School Drugs Pack*, Healthwise, 1995.

Combes and Craft, *Special Health*, HEA 1989.
A Health Education source book for teachers of pupils with learning difficulties.

DrugSense, Hertfordshire LEA and New Media, 1998.
CD-ROM with content-regulating facility, manual and lesson plans. (PC and Macintosh.) Ground-breaking resource for 9–13 year-olds.

Foster, *Answers*, Collins, 1996. Pack 1: 7–9, Pack 2: 9–11.
General PSHE resources, with colourful posters and exercises.

Learning for Life, Grampian Police/Shell Education Service, 1999.
An interactive CD-ROM providing pupil exercises and teacher guidance for promoting health, safety and personal and social development which foster good citizenship.

Moon, *Skills for the Primary School Child*, in particular volumes 1 and 2, TACADE, 1990.
Skills-based PSHE resources for pupils aged 5–11.

Wetton and Collins, *Ourselves*, BBC Educational Publishing, 1998.
A package of classroom materials, produced in association with the Health Education Board for Scotland, for use independently or with the *Ourselves* unit in the BBC series *Watch*.

Talk Health, Health Promotion Wales, 1997.
A resource for primary schools which represents a developmental programme of drugs education from age 5 to age 11.

Williams, Wetton and Moon, *Health for Life* Books 1 and 2, Nelson, 1989.
General planning guides for Health Education for pupils aged 5–11.
Book 2 has a major section, 'The World of Drugs'.

Other useful publications

Chapman, *Drug Issues for Schools* (2nd Edition), ISDD, 1995.

Clements and Jack, *Peer Led Drug Education*, Daniels, 1994.
Handbook of peer-led education, training 15 and 16 year-old pupils to offer structured drugs education to their younger peers.

Drug Abuse Briefing: 7th Edition, ISDD, 1999.
New editions are published periodically.

McFadyean, *Drugs Wise*, Icon Books, 1997.

England

The following documents are available free from DfEE Publications Unit. Telephone: 0845 602 2260:

Drug Prevention and Schools, Circular 4/95, DfEE, 1995.

Drug Education: Curriculum Guidance for Schools, SCAA, 1995.

Supporting Pupils with Medical Needs, DfEE/DoH Good Practice Guide: DfEE, 1996.

Drug Education in Schools, OFSTED, 1997.

Protecting Young People: Good Practice in Drug Education in Schools and the Youth Service, DfEE, 1998.

The Right Choice: Guidance on Selecting Drug Education Materials for Schools, SCODA/DEF, 1998.

The Right Approach: Quality Standards in Drug Education, SCODA, 1999.

The Right Responses: Managing and Making Policy for Drug-related Incidents in Schools, SCODA, 1999.

Wales

Drug Misuse: Prevention and Schools, Welsh Office Circular 54/95.

Supporting Pupils with Medical Needs in Schools, Welsh Office Circular 34/97.

Supporting Pupils with Medical Needs: Good Practice Guide, Welsh Office, December 1997.

Scotland

A Guide to Child Health in the Primary School by Dr Sandy Irvine, HEBS. ISBN: 1 902 030 00 1.

The Curriculum Guidelines for 5–14 series of documents refer to Health Education in *Environmental Studies and Personal and Social Development*.

The 1998 update of the *Health Education for Living Project (HELP)* guidelines contain references to drugs education. Scottish CCC. Telephone: 01382 455053.

Smoking Policies for Scottish Schools – An Action Plan, HEBS/ASH (Scotland), 1994. ISBN: 0 952 0673 1 5.

Guidelines for the Management of Drug Misuse in Schools – a draft consultation produced by the School Drug Safety Team.
Scottish Executive, 1999 ISBN: 0 7480 8270 0